# Visualize Your Teaching

T0383578

*Visualize Your Teaching* offers a unique way of helping educators see their own teaching so they can strengthen their practice.

Author Kyle Ezell uses a series of simple but compelling black and white graphics to take you through teaching's parts, flows, and signals. He demonstrates that it's important to be aware of what's happening when playing distinctly different *parts* as you teach, depending on the context. *Flows* connect parts together over a lesson. He shows how to visualize the impact of how flows connect over a range of circumstances. You also need to be aware of how you respond to many different *signals* that appear, pushing and pulling the lesson plan.

Appropriate for teachers of all grade levels and subject areas, the book provides teaching scenario prompts for you to practice playing all the parts through self-observation and opportunities for you to diagram your own teaching. As you work through the pages, you'll be able to visualize your performance the way athletes do, becoming more in tune with yourself. With this book as your batting cage, you will be increasing your impact on students in no time!

Once a solidly marginal teacher, **Kyle Ezell**, EdD, became an inductee into The Ohio State University's prestigious Academy of Teaching, receiving many awards for his role as an educator. A professor of city and regional planning in Ohio State's Knowlton School of Architecture in the College of Engineering since 2005, Dr. Ezell serves as a Faculty Foundation, Impact, and Transformation (FIT) Program mentor for new and developing teachers at Ohio State and as a Senior Affiliate with the university's Michael V. Drake Institute for Teaching and Learning, and enjoys consulting K-12 educators in visualizing their teaching.

# Visualize Your Teaching

## Understand Your Style and Increase Your Impact

Kyle Ezell

Routledge
Taylor & Francis Group

NEW YORK AND LONDON

First published 2023
by Routledge
605 Third Avenue, New York, NY 10158

and by Routledge
4 Park Square, Milton Park, Abingdon, Oxon, OX14 4RN

*Routledge is an imprint of the Taylor & Francis Group, an informa business*

*Library of Congress Cataloging-in-Publication Data*
Names: Ezell, Kyle, author.
Title: Visualize your teaching : understand your style and increase your
impact / Kyle Ezell.
Description: New York, NY : Routledge, 2023. | Series: Routledge eye on
education | Includes bibliographical references. | Identifiers: LCCN 2022039404
(print) | LCCN 2022039405 (ebook) | ISBN 9781032416885 (paperback) |
ISBN 9781032418896 (hardback) | ISBN 9781003360230 (ebook)
Subjects: LCSH: Reflective teaching. | Effective teaching.
Classification: LCC LB1025.3 .E97 2023 (print) | LCC LB1025.3 (ebook) |
DDC 371.102--dc23/eng/20220930
LC record available at https://lccn.loc.gov/2022039404
LC ebook record available at https://lccn.loc.gov/2022039405

ISBN: 9781032418896 (hbk)
ISBN: 9781032416885 (pbk)
ISBN: 9781003360230 (ebk)

DOI: 10.4324/9781003360230

Typeset in Palatino
by KnowledgeWorks Global Ltd.

# Contents

# About the Author

**Kyle Ezell,** EdD, once a solidly marginal teacher, became an inductee into The Ohio State University's prestigious Academy of Teaching, receiving many awards for his role as an educator. Since 2005, he has been a professor of city and regional planning in Ohio State's Knowlton School of Architecture in the College of Engineering. Dr. Ezell serves as a Faculty Foundation, Impact, and Transformation (FIT) Program mentor for new and developing teachers at Ohio State and as a Senior Affiliate with the university's Michael V. Drake Institute for Teaching and Learning, and enjoys consulting K-12 educators in visualizing their teaching.

# Foreword

By Doug Sershen, Manager, Operations and Advancement, Knowlton School, Ohio State University

Through my role supporting appointment, promotion, and tenure processes at the Austin E. Knowlton School of Architecture, I enjoyed numerous opportunities to speak with Kyle Ezell about his goal of becoming "the best teacher at Ohio State," a tall feat considering his rocky start as a teacher. Our initial conversation on the topic stemmed from his frustration and concern over early-career annual reviews identifying spotty, disappointing teaching.

I wandered into Kyle's office shortly after that review and left an hour or so later. Kyle told me he believed that time was too short for incremental improvements; if he needed to put in the work, he committed to leaving his marginal teaching behind and begin cracking the code to become the best teacher at the University.

And he did.

It's a common occurrence for junior faculty who have chosen education as a career in part because of the impact great teachers have had on them personally, but then are distressed to discover that their own skills as educators are failing to meet the needs of their students. Distress turns to shock when in "that talk" with leadership about their qualifications for promotion, questions are asked about their teaching.

Several years later, I helped prepare the materials nominating Kyle for the University's highest teaching award, an Ohio State University Alumni Award for Distinguished Teaching. The nomination referenced Kyle's pedagogical creativity and commitment to experiential learning. Pointing to the top teaching award he had recently received from Ohio State's College of Engineering, it included comments from former students, such as: "The professor is passionate, and thinks and teaches in a unique way..." The University presents this during a surprise visit by the Provost and other top administrators to the winner's classroom. After his surprise visit, Kyle stopped by my office to proclaim that he could "die happy."

Now, with *Visualize Your Teaching*, Kyle shares how he turned his teaching around through visualization techniques and creating diagrams illustrating the roles teachers play in the classroom. His simple drawings linked workflows that combine the discrete components of effective teaching and identify warning signals that often derail lessons.

*Visualize Your Teaching* will be essential for teachers at any level, K-12 to college, to anyone committed to becoming their best, or even *the* best.

# Preface

Once upon a time, I was a solidly marginal teacher. Frustrated and disillusioned, I thought it might be helpful to watch other teachers and maybe find inspiration. Only a few hours of observing two classes began my teaching transformation journey and eventually created this book to share how you can do the same.

I peeked in on a class where a teacher faced a chalkboard, seemingly on a mission to cover equations over every square inch. This "educator" frantically clicked his chalk—*click-click-click-click-click*—equations emerging— creating a squiggly chalk dust wake. He called out the numbers in his monotonous, choppy voice that complemented the chalk scrapes, furiously scribbling symbols, never looking back from the blackboard or attempting to connect with his students.

I leaned further into the classroom to get a glimpse, then snuck a seat in the back row and instantly noticed how most students were physically present but certainly not really "there." While some students' heads pointed down in frantic notetaking, trying to keep up with the clicks, too many wore blank faces, and some seemed to be working on other courses; several were chatting, a few wore headphones, and I noticed one student filing her nails.

I forced myself to sit in this class until the end, miserable, witnessing educational malfeasance. As the chalk dust cloud grew, the teacher did not take time to notice (more likely, he did not care) whether his teaching was positively impacting his students and whether they paid any attention to his overwhelming deluge of content.

This terrible teacher's focus—exclusively on content—revealed his uncaring self-centered approach. Although I'm sure he thought he was doing a great job, as an observer, it seemed he believed the course revolved around getting lost in his bliss, alone with his chalk, enjoying the sound of his voice, students be damned.

Recalling my appalling teaching evaluations and negative comments from my students, I wondered, "Could this teacher be me?"

Continuing my quest to watch teachers, I became drawn toward a loud, echoey, collective gasp of a big crowd, followed by laughter ricocheting against the cinderblock hallway walls. Lively and unusual, the sounds drew me into the room. The instructor, arms waving in the air, wearing a cheeky smile, and responding to the students' reactions, settled into her performance. She talked about something, but I didn't care what she was saying—I was immediately mesmerized, carefully scanning the students' attentiveness—she set up a feeling.

Looking around the classroom revealed awake, wide-eyed, fully engaged students. I saw several expressions of wonder as the students' erect spines leaned into the teacher's words. Transfixed, I felt the room's ecstatic-electric-eccentric mood building up in a frantic tempo.

By the time I stole a seat in an empty row in the back, this instructor had suddenly shifted the tone of the course to a focused, much more contemplative, quiet setting, a specific and intentional change in her teaching rhythm. She put the students to work, and I watched them remain engaged in a new, calm, dynamic, and purposeful way.

*I was amazed.* I could tell these students had their minds set ablaze. Still etched in my soul, this incredible teacher's class made me want to figure out how to light my students' minds up as she did.

The students' experience means everything! I realized great teachers create and shift the tones of their classrooms, noticing how students respond and understanding the experience they establish. I learned how best teachers manage their tempos and volumes and how they change their students' reactions. Brilliant teachers know how and when they behave and move in one way instead of others and how little decisions profoundly shape their students' experience.

# Visualizing Across Our Profession

Soon after this epiphany, I started visualizing my teaching. "Seeing" made all the difference in my transformation, but I wondered, because I was a college professor, if this might also apply to K-12 teaching.

To find out, I enrolled in a graduate-level K-12 course on classroom observational leadership and lesson planning. There, I realized I had uncovered something universal to the broader teaching profession. Though, of course, there are major differences in many aspects of teaching different students and levels, I found out that K-12 and college teachers don't vary as much as I thought: that course confirmed the importance of harnessing educational intuition and making sense of the complex situations and contexts that can enhance or destroy the most thoughtful, detailed lesson plans.

My higher education colleagues also agree grasping nuances and knowing what to do with these hard-to-talk-about elements of teaching I feature in this book can make or break careers since, until now, they existed only "in the air." It doesn't matter which student level you teach; what you're about to learn works for any teacher who teaches kindergarten or college or vocational school or Sunday School because it's not about teaching finger painting or calculus. It's not about content at all. Your successful future as an educator requires making meaning of the intangibles. I'll show you how.

## Why You Can Trust Me

Thrust into a university classroom, I knew I'd be successful because I thought I had a "teacher's personality." But almost immediately after I started teaching my first class at Ohio State University, many of my students revolted directly from my class to my Department Head's office in a mutiny of dissatisfaction and strident complaints. I know of at least one other rebellion though there were probably more. And it was clear most students did not respect me or take me seriously.

I got lucky in a few classes, but my teaching did not improve much over the first few years, and I became very frustrated. Too many student evaluations upset and appalled me, and the collection of profoundly negative comments deeply hurt my feelings and confidence. A warning light for taking immediate action came when my boss confronted me over their concern about perhaps not being able to "tell a story and plot a timeline of continuous improvement" in support of potential promotion opportunities for me because of my teaching performance.

*Warning!* The following may come across as pompous, but there's no way around sharing my teaching credentials to explain why you should trust me. Implementing this book's strategy took me from embarrassing and deplorable student reviews and closed-door reprimand conversations to spectacular teaching heights. I'm astounded by my (dramatic) teaching turnaround, so here goes:

I'm recognized as one of the most distinguished teachers in my college, also university wide at colossal Ohio State University. I received the (very) top Award for Distinguished Teaching. (The head of the awards committee informed my teaching associate and me during a surprise classroom visit to present this award that my ranking was #1 of thousands of eligible teachers. The best day of my life was being celebrated on the field at a Buckeye football game as a recipient of this award.) In a medal ceremony, OSU inducted me into its prestigious Academy of Teaching. During its commencement with tens of thousands of attendees, I am called out with an exclusive group of a few teachers wearing the silver medallion acknowledged as one of the university's outstanding educators. I also was the sole winner of The Ohio State College of Engineering's Distinguished Faculty Award for Outstanding Teaching; the Faculty Award for University Community Members Who Have Made a Positive Influence on Ohio State Students; the Award for Outstanding Commitment to Student Education, The Ohio State University Faculty Award for Excellence in Community-Based Scholarship; appointed to Senior Affiliate serving and consulting OSU's Michael V. Drake Institute for Teaching and Learning. OSU selected me as one of a few mentors for training new and developing teachers. And putting my doctorate in education to good use, my teaching course load includes leading PhD practicums to teach future teachers how to be great educators! *(Whew!)*

I still can't believe it, and it feels like a miracle considering my unstable beginnings. I know how self-congratulatory putting a long string of teaching accolades in a book sounds, and I can't help but get ill when I read it, but it's what happened to me by activating the method you will soon learn, and why a world leader in education publishing such as Routledge decided to take this book.

It wasn't a miracle, though. My design-oriented background caused me to stumble on the power of "seeing" my teaching. My secret until now, this book's simple roadmap can help you see yours and become your best.

# Introduction
## "The Feeling" Students Get from Your Teaching

I cracked the code to becoming a great teacher.

I wrote this book to share my secret with you.

Maybe you already consider yourself an excellent teacher—perhaps even the best in your building or campus. You might be coming clean with yourself as a marginal teacher like I did in my past life when my boss warned me about my less than stellar teaching, and you hope to turn everything around to benefit your students. No matter where you are in your career, who you teach, or where you work, I will help you transform your teaching.

Most teachers (especially new ones) don't understand that the key to becoming their best starts when realizing excellent teaching has nothing to do with content. You and every other teacher have access to content and similar lesson plans. Even if you curate the highest quality content, it's not enough. Becoming a great teacher also isn't only about learning strategies; if you research and practice the highest-impact evidence-based ways students learn, so can every other educator. If brilliant teaching only means delivering content and executing evidence-based teaching strategies, robots could step in.

DOI: 10.4324/9781003360230-1

The most effective teachers deeply understand and "feel" their teaching, responding, and shifting to quickly meet changing individual needs and those of the entire class. They have a handle on the details and nuances of how they respond and react—manage and conduct—modify and connect—the multiple complex human interactions they encounter in every lesson. Doing all this means continuously visualizing their teaching, including confronting, understanding, and embracing unique rhythms that make up their signature style and, especially, harnessing the intangibles of teaching. This book breaks down these intangibles for you to effectively and efficiently visualize your teaching: the *parts* teachers play, the *flows* teachers choose to connect the parts, and responding to or waving off the many informing or alerting *signals*.

## Parts

Eminent educators must be aware of "playing" distinctly different **parts** when they teach. Knowing the contexts and characteristics of each part you play lifts your foundational awareness beyond the content you deliver, helping you more clearly visualize and therefore understand your teaching. In Chapter 1, you'll learn how to spot and detail different ways you engage with students, "your parts." [Please be mindful, though, not to confuse identifying and describing the parts you play with acting from a script. Actors try to become someone else; as a teacher, you stay you.]

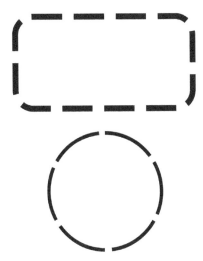

**FIGURE 0.1** Parts

## Flows

*Flows* connect parts. The most effective teachers know the impacts of how flows connect over a range of circumstances. When playing one of the twelve parts I'll introduce in Chapter 1, I know I'll soon be playing another, shifting again and maybe swinging back to the one I started with, creating a string of connected parts. I sense when flows feel seamless and recognize when I chose a flow that didn't string my parts together smoothly. Later in Chapter 2, you can study my flows diagrams. I'll show you how to visualize your teaching so you can create your own, identifying your complementary and conflicting flows and how decisions for combining flows contribute to exemplary (and also awful) teaching.

**FIGURE 0.2** Flows

# Signals

Understanding how you treat sudden information that pushes and pulls (and sometimes derails) your lesson (i.e., *signals*) helps you become more able to visualize your teaching. In Chapter 2, through sensing, spotting, and responding to signals, you'll grow your ability to know what to do. In no time, you'll prime your instincts for how, when, and why a sudden indicator makes you modify or abandon a part currently being played, decide which part to play next, and predict how it affects existing flows, adjusting immediately.

**FIGURE 0.3** A signal

# Teaching as Performing

Excellent teachers know the power of visualizing their performance in the classroom, but not like actors perform—*as athletes do*. Star softball players don't indiscriminately swing at every ball; they "see" themselves playing many parts that specify how or if they swing—a pinch hitter, a bunter, an intentional walker, and all the others. "Seeing" their performances before they take the field, the most talented athletes connect the parts they play, monitoring and "feeling" in or out of their optimal performance zones, shifting as necessary. Visualizing keeps them aware of threats and opportunities to instantly make decisions on potential (and essential!) changes to reach their optimal performance. The best teachers do this, too!

Consider this book as your "batting cage" that, with proper time spent, will ramp up your teaching performance using visualization techniques. Through pinpointing and characterizing the once abstract teaching parts you play, you'll manage those until now intangible flows that connect your parts and the range of in-your-face and ethereal signals that exclaim, "change your direction!" You'll learn how to perform as an excellent educator, adjusting as circumstances change, and split-second shifting to keep students' attention so they can meet your learning outcomes expectations. You'll become a superstar teacher by continuously visualizing your performances, honing your classroom reflexes, and educational intuition.

Notably, becoming an excellent educator does not mean innately possessing some kind of "secret sauce" for teaching success. Neither does it have to do with personality; your coolest teacher may not have been particularly impactful. No matter your personality type, it's not about you; instead, it's how to enhance your awareness and reflexively alter your performance to meet your students' ever-changing needs. Anyone can learn the power of visualizing their teaching and succeed.

# Drawing's Energy

Staples in our lesson plans, drawing, diagramming, and doodling help students learn. Now it's time for educators to practice strengthening our imagination, creating illustrations worth a thousand words. Hand-to-mind thinking boosts your ability to develop your teaching rhythm, helping you sense what's happening now, what could or might occur, and the best ways to respond and react. I'll show you how drawing builds energy into your practice and strengthens your muscle memory, enabling you to conduct and connect brilliantly.[1]

Ms. Mia, a third-grade teacher, discusses how she teaches using this book's diagrams as she leads a remote in-service session.

**FIGURE 0.4** Ms. Mia

Mr. Jamisal, a high school geometry teacher, shares his simple, fun, doodled diagram explaining "his teaching."

**FIGURE 0.5** Mr. Jamisal

Dr. Deutsch, a professor of sociology, displays and explains her general classroom tempo flow strategy for the intro course she taught today.

**FIGURE 0.6** Dr. Deutsch

See how drawings need not look professional or pretty? By the way, this book features diagrams I digitized from only-intelligible-to-me hand-sketched versions, and they're far from beautiful and nowhere near perfect—but they're perfect to me! The only requirement is that the drawer understands what they created and can easily explain them.

# Teaching Charrettes

In addition to being an educator, I'm a city planning practitioner with a lot of experience facilitating many creative, engaging meetings called "charrettes." Charrette, meaning "cart," comes from 19th-century Paris and describes intense community workshops where people imagine, then visually share conceptualizations for ideal buildings, streets, and parks.[2] However, before the ideal communities envisioned by participants can manifest, charrettes begin with establishing a baseline for a community's existing conditions, where participants doodle, sketch, and diagram what they see in the present day. Their drawings don't have to be pretty or even legible as long as the drawer thoroughly solidifies ideas, explaining them in ways for everyone involved to understand.

*This book's method brings the existing conditions aspect of charrettes to the field of education.* Just like communities, teachers can't improve without first understanding what's happening right now in their teaching practice! Keen awareness of your existing teaching conditions powers future improvements in your evolving practice. This awareness requires teachers to watch their details, and I'll show you how in this book.

**FIGURE 0.7** Ms. Benson and her colleague at an in-service charrette

Ms. Benson, a kindergarten teacher sharing her drawing with a colleague in a charrette, illustrates how visualizing and sharing our parts, flows, and signals can add value to in-service or faculty retreat activities and, ultimately, students.

You can use this book as a framework for programming active, creative, transformative (and different!) professional growth experiences from small community practice sessions to large school- or district-wide events. Charrettes are also helpful in confronting pressing topics and specific needs so participants can learn how they and others handle them and collect ideas.

# Self-Observation and Teacher Intuition

Self-observation, or watching yourself teach in your imagination to know better how your decisions influence your students' experience, likely sounds odd though it has long been part of reflective practice in education.[3] At first, assessing your teaching in your mind will likely feel a bit strange as you interact with imaginary students. Still, detailing your decisions and behaviors through visualizing provides the foundation for the method I introduce in this book. Knowing your specifics helps deconstruct how you teach, which is essential for effective diagramming of your teaching.

Watching myself teach in my mind and identifying how I play parts, manage flows, and treat signals—then make meaning of my choices, and draw "my teaching"—resembles a layperson's application of math's category theory. Instead of looking at things by their intrinsic characteristics, you can learn a lot by looking at how they are related to each other to better understand everything in context rather than in isolation. Through organizing the complexities of your teaching, you turn large quantities of information into easily understandable units whose relationships vary; you do this when identifying details of your decisions and how they affect your students.

In the context of visualizing your teaching, category theory says:

◆ Every teacher's parts, flows, and signals have a context.
◆ Each is appropriate in some contexts and not in others.
◆ Each should be examined with the others and not by themselves.
◆ Creating abstract visuals makes it easier to define how teachers teach by examining the relationships between their parts, flows, and signals.[4]

I'm not a mathematician; however, though far from an exact theoretical match, these tenants of category theory generally explain my thought processes in this book.

Naturally, self-observation of your teaching relates to building intuition. In 2006, Leonard Waks, an American philosophy scholar, called intuition a forgotten gift in education and suggested renewing interest in educational intuition. Waks wrote a chapter "Intuition in Education" in the *Philosophy of Education*, where he lays the foundation for what I build on and put into material practice in this book:

> Each educator is presented from minute to minute with information-rich circumstances, under various institutional constraints, which present innumerable opportunities for generating both general and specific educational value... Experienced teachers ... have a rich body of experience that guides them in scanning their immediate circumstances for opportunities and then rapidly and flexibly responding without the explicit mediation of consciousness to generate educational value.
>
> (Waks, 2006, p. 385)

Waks believes we strengthen intuition through "concentrated experience." I do not claim to be an expert in cognitive psychology. Still, I contend that by becoming familiar with the details—*especially the visualized details*—of our parts, flows, and signals with frequent self-observation, teachers gain much more concentrated experience than teachers who don't take the time to self-evaluate their work comprehensively.

Since intuition occurs in your mind (and does so without the explicit mediation of consciousness), watching yourself teach in your mind develops a knack for understanding nuances. What seems to be happening now?

What's happening under the surface, and what could or might occur?

Educators grasp the importance of harnessing educational intuition. Sipman et al.'s 2019 qualitative research study published in the *British Educational Research Journal* conducted focus groups of school districts and a teacher training college in The Netherlands. Participants shared ideas on the possibility of developing teachers' intuition. Main themes included in representative narratives from the conversations beautifully sum up what we all know:

1. Intangible/intuitive elements of teaching are important in the educational process.
2. The intangibles help us better understand and deliver student differentiation.
3. The intangibles are the "heart of our job."

---

### "Intuition"

My contribution to educational intuition is how teachers respond to the human parts of our practice that don't involve the usual mechanics. Still, unless you're a seasoned teacher keeping up with evidence-based learning, going with a gut feeling about a fantastic lesson plan or lesson strategy is far from ideal—we absolutely should follow the science (Weinstein et al., 2019). For now, try to forget about science. (I know it's hard!) To keep things easy, when I refer to intuition in this book, please remember I'm talking about flash decisions on how we choose to behave when we're with our students that differentiate us from robots.

You'll soon engage in a more tangible way to develop intuition when you teach. You'll learn the best ways to respond and react—becoming better able to sense and "see," eventually doing all of this without having to think, making informed, flash decisions. Also, while the rational aspects of our teaching remain vital, enhancing your educational intuition requires temporarily throwing them out, including consideration of your expert topical content (e.g., English, History, and all the others) and specific items in your lesson plans.

*Don't overthink this!* Keep these grounding ideas in mind that your parts, flows, and signals turn theory into instructional practice and that you will soon become an exceptional (or even more fantastic) teacher.

---

### Other Ways to "See"

"Watching" your teaching means visualizing—*imagining*. We all imagine. Still, how we make meaning of what we imagine differs. I am a highly visual learner—doodling and drawing power my mind. I love employing graphics, diagrams, charts, maps, flashcards, and pictures—to better see and understand more thoroughly, including how I teach. Tactile thinkers and learners will likely enjoy working with paper and markers as they visualize. However, the audial-oriented might find ways to tell stories orally to explain their teaching instead of diagramming, perhaps creating recordings to tell their teaching stories. So, after "watching" yourself through self-observation, feel free to process your information however it works best for your preferences and abilities, even though this book spotlights drawing.

---

# An Uncovering

Immediately after introducing and explaining parts, flows, and signals, teachers I mentor say, "Wow, of course!" because it's an uncovering. But this is not new! Though they likely would not be able to explain how experienced educators eventually learn these previously nameless, intangible, abstract, hard-to-describe (stuck in the ether until now) variables that I converted into more digestible, concrete concepts. However, whether new or seasoned, you are already a teacher forever changed; simply being aware that parts, flows, and signals exist will soon be transformative.

Any teacher who stops reading can already use this new awareness to identify various parts they play, at least one or two flows that connect those parts, and how they react to signals. *But keep going!* Following my directions, you will quickly develop an automatic, keen instinct for how, when, and why to modify or abandon a part, decide which part to play next, predict how it affects existing flows, and watch out for the flurry of signals to make positive impacts on students and propel your career, just as doing this did for me.

# How to Get Ready

The following items and thoughts to ponder will help you prepare for your transformational journey to becoming a more well-rounded, effective educator.

## Gather Drawing Materials

You'll need something to draw with and on. Grabbing a sketchbook and using thin markers remains my favorite way, a place you can combine your sketches, notes, and journaling. A technical device with a drawing surface works great, too. Go more casual if you wish with an old spiral-bound tablet, or even grab a few napkins. I've also enjoyed using posterboards, and when I started diagramming my teaching, I did it mainly on a whiteboard hanging in my office. I strongly recommend working in a sketchbook where you can see your progress over time and reflect through the pages.

If you're diagramming in groups such as in communities of practice, in-service sessions, or faculty retreats, try big markers on regular poster paper with masking tape or ready-to-apply adhesives for wall hanging so everyone can see and understand each other's teaching, glean ideas, and discuss.

---

### Don't Worry!

Many of my students become anxious when I tell them they must draw. Call it "doodling." (Or "scribbling" so it will seem less intimidating.) It bears repeating that your diagrams don't have to be perfect or even legible as long as you solidify your ideas, allowing you to explain them to others clearly. The point of this exercise isn't about the quality of the things you draw; "seeing" your teaching, however scribbly, builds your relationship with yourself as a teacher.

---

## Adopt, Then Modify My Visuals

The last thing I want to do is tell you exactly how you should teach! However, as a seasoned teacher, I am confident that the parts, flows, and signals I identified in this book generally represent those played by every teacher, but every teacher customizes the specs. For ease and clarity, start by employing my already built-out examples and "watch" yourself to understand your teaching better and interpret your style. As you continue your journey, you'll naturally modify my start, adding and naming new parts, personalizing your flows and signals, and customizing how you graphically display and explain your teaching.

## Student/s and Student's/s'

I made this stylistic decision to include singular and plural words in one because we play parts, establish flows, and watch for and respond to signals with individual students, groups, and entire classrooms.

## Follow the Steps in Order

Prepare to be stepped through a process I synthesized. Be ready for me to engage you with simple, direct prompts to help you along the way. Please work through each page without skipping because each concept builds. Sometimes I'll give you prompts to spark your imagination. Other times, I'll introduce ideas and ask you to contemplate diagrams or use storytelling to explain scenarios to help you understand your parts, flows, and signals. You'll soon be actively imagining yourself in various teaching situations, documenting your details so you can identify and understand your parts. Then you'll make meaning of and diagram (or scribble!) your flows and signals and find out how to put all of this to work in your classroom.

**Let's Go!**

# References

## 1. Outcomes-Based Benefits of Drawing/ Hand-Eye/Visual Learning

Ainsworth, S. E., & Scheiter, K. K. (January 13, 2021). Learning by drawing visual representation: Potential, purposes, and practical implications. *Current Directions in Psychological Science* *30*(1), 61–67. DOI: 10.1177/0963721420979582.

Andrade, J. (2009). What does doodling do? *Applied Cognitive Psychology.* *24*(1), 100–106. DOI: 10.1002/acp.1561.

Chang et al. (2019). The features of norms formed in constructing student-generated drawings to explain physics. *Won Journal: International Journal of Science Education.* *42*(8), 1362–1387. DOI: 10.1080/09500693.2020.1762138.

Cooper, M. M., Stieff, M., & DeSutter, D. (2017). Sketching the invisible to predict the visible: From drawing to modeling in chemistry. *Topics in Cognitive Science.* *9*(4), 902–920. DOI: 10.1111/tops.12285.

Cromley, J. G., Du, Y., & Dane, A. P. (2019). Drawing-to-learn: Does meta-analysis show differences between technology-based drawing and paper-and-pencil drawing? *Journal of Science Education and Technology.* *29*(2), 216–229. DOI: 10.1007/s10956-019-09807-6.

Fernandes, M. A., Wammes, J. D., & Meade, M. E. (2018). The surprisingly powerful influence of drawing on memory. *Current Directions in Psychological Science.* *27*(5), 302–308. DOI: https://doi.org/10.1177/0963721418755385.

Fiorella, L., & Kuhlmann, S. (2020). Creating drawings enhances learning by teaching. *Journal of Educational Psychology.* *112*(4), 811–822. DOI: https://doi.org/10.1037/edu0000392.

Fiorella, L., & Zhang, Q. (2018). Drawing boundary conditions for learning by drawing. *Educational Psychology Review.* *30*(3), 1115–1137. DOI: https://doi.org/10.1007/s10648-018-9444-8.

Heijnes, D., van Joolingen, W., & Leenaars, F. (2018). Stimulating scientific reasoning with drawing-based modeling. *Journal of Science Education and Technology.* *27*(1), 45–56. DOI: https://doi.org/10.1007/s10956-017-9707-z.

Jenkinson, J. (2017). The role of craft-based knowledge in the design of dynamic visualizations. In R. Lowe & R. Ploetzner (Eds.), *Learning from dynamic visualization* (1st ed.). New York, NY: Springer.

Kohnle, A., Ainsworth, S. E., & Passante, G. (2020). Sketching to support visual learning with interactive tutorials. *Physical Review Physics Education Research, 16*(2). DOI: https://doi.org/10.1103/PhysRevPhysEducRes.16.020139.

Kohen et al. (2022). Self-efficacy and problem-solving skills in mathematics: The effect of instruction-based dynamic versus static visualization. *Interactive Learning Environments. 30*(4), 759. DOI: 10.1080/10494820.2019.1683588.

Lardi, C., & Leopold, C. (2022). Effects of interactive teacher-generated drawings on students' understanding of plate tectonics. *Instructional Science. 50*(2), 273. DOI: 10.1007/s11251-021-09567-0.

Larkin, J., & Simon, H. (1987). Why a diagram is (sometimes) worth ten thousand words. *Cognitive Science. 11*(1), 65–100. DOI: https://doi.org/10.1111/j.1551-6708.1987.tb00863.x.

Ploetzenr, R., & Bryer, B. (2017). *Learning from dynamic visualization*. New York, NY: Springer. DOI: 10.1007/978-3-319-56204-9_15.

Quillin, K., & Thomas, S. (2015). Drawing-to-learn: A framework for using drawings to promote model-based reasoning in biology. *CBE—Life Sciences Education. 14*(1). DOI: https://doi.org/10.1187/cbe.14-08-0128.

Ryan, S., & Steiff, R. (2019). Drawing for assessing learning outcomes in chemistry. *Journal of Chemical Education. 96*(9), 1813. DOI: 10.1021/acs.jchemed.9b00361.

Schmidgall, S. P., Eitel, A., & Scheiter, K. (2019). Why do learners who draw perform well? Investigating the role of visualization, generation and externalization in learner-generated drawing. *Learning and Instruction. 60*, 138–153. DOI: https://doi.org/10.1016/j.learninstruc.2018.01.006.

Shatri, K. (2017). The use of visualization in teaching and learning process for developing critical thinking of students. *European Journal of Social Science Education and Research. 4*(1), 71–74. DOI: https://doi.org/10.26417/ejser.v9i1.p71-74.

Steiff, M. (2017). Drawing for promoting learning and engagement with dynamic visualizations. In R. Lowe, & R. Ploetzner (Eds.), *Learning from dynamic visualization* (1st ed., pp. 69–93). New York, NY: Springer.

Steiff, M., & Desutter, D. (2021). Sketching, not representational competence, predicts improved science learning. *Journal of Research in Science Teaching 58*(1), 128. DOI: 10.1002/tea.21650.

Steiff, M. (2019). Improving learning outcomes in secondary chemistry with visualization-supported inquiry activities. *Journal of Chemical Education. 96*(7), 1300. DOI: 10.1021/acs.jchemed.9b00205.

Van Meter, P., & Firetto, C. (2013). Cognitive model of drawing construction. In G. Schraw, M. T. McCrudden, & D. Robinson (Eds.), *Learning through visual displays* (pp. 247–280). Charlotte, NC: Information Age Publishing.

Yip, K. (2006). Self-reflection in reflective practice: A note of caution. *British Journal of Social Work. 36*, 777–788.

## 2. Charrettes

Lennertz et al. (2014). *The charrette handbook*. London: Taylor and Francis.

## 3. Educational Intuition and Self-Observation

Hough, L. (2020). A teacher's intuition: Teachers rely on it, often dozens of times every day in their classrooms. Sometimes it works; sometimes it doesn't. It usually gets easier to trust with experience. *Harvard Ed Magazine*. Cambridge, MA: Harvard University. Retrieved from https://www.gse.harvard.edu/news/ed/20/05/teacher%E2%80%99s-intuition

Richards, J. C. (1990). The teacher as self-observer. In J. C. Richards (Ed.), *The language teaching matrix*. New York, NY: Cambridge University Press.

Schon D. A. (1983). *The reflective practitioner: How professionals think in action*. New York, NY: Basic Books.

Sipman et al. (2019). The role of intuition in pedagogical tact: Educator views. *British Educational Research Journal. 45*(6), 1186–1202. DOI: 10.1002/berj.3557.

Tomasino, D. (2011). The heart in intuition: Tools for cultivating intuitive intelligence. In M. Sinclair (Ed.), *Handbook of intuition research* (pp. 247–260). Cheltenham: Edward Elgar.

Valle, A. (2017). Teachers' intuitive interaction competence and how to learn it. *European Journal of Teacher Education. 40*(2), 246–256. DOI: 10.1080/02619768.2017.1295033.

Vagle, M. (2011). Critically-oriented pedagogical tact: Learning about and through our compulsions as teacher educators. *Teaching Education. 22*(4), 413–426.

van Manen, M. (2015). *Pedagogical tact: Knowing what to do when you don't know what to do*. New York, NY: Routledge.

Waks, L. J. (2006). Intuition in education: Teaching and learning without thinking. In. Vokey, D. (Ed.), *Philosophy of Education*, 2006, (pp. 379–388). Philosophy of Education Society.

Weinstein et al. (2019). *Understanding how we learn: A visual guide*. London: Routledge.

# 4. Category Theory

Cheng, E. (2017). Category theory in real life. Lambda World Conference, Cadiz, Spain. Available from: https://www.youtube.com/watch?v=ho7oagHeqNc

Fong, B., & Spivak, D. (2019). *An invitation to applied category theory: Seven sketches in compositionality* (1st ed.). Cambridge: Cambridge University Press.

# 1

# Parts: 12 That Teachers Play (Run through 50 Performances)

All teachers "play" parts. This chapter will help you visualize your teaching to identify and understand how you play them. A way to categorize what we do when we teach, parts represent a collection of specific characteristics for your decisions and how you behave. The various contexts of teaching require you to play multiple parts, and these contexts change frequently. Please be mindful not to confuse identifying and describing the parts you play with acting from a script. Actors try to become someone else; teachers don't. In this chapter, you'll identify and describe the parts you play and name the precise ways you respond to classroom situations.

DOI: 10.4324/9781003360230-2

# Framing and Drilling Parts

The first step in this process is to know the difference between a Framing Part and a Drilling Part.

**FIGURE 1.1** A Framing Part

Framing Parts frame a topic or a situation, setting a particular tone I sometimes refer to as "the feeling." Situationally dependent, Framing Parts congratulate, take control, deliver consequences, provide freedom, and other student needs, establishing classroom (or one-on-one) expectations. (Significantly, Framing Parts do not directly contribute subject-related content.) I expect to play a Framing Part at the beginning and end of a lesson or conversation, but I know anytime could require a significant tone shift.

**FIGURE 1.2** A Drilling Part

*Drilling Parts* drill down into subject-related content and assignments, such as lecturing and learning activities, set by a Framing Part's established tone. Different situations and circumstances require a specific Drilling Part.

# Playing Parts in Practice

To understand Framing Parts and Drilling Parts in practice, imagine yourself as a student observer of Mr. Misery and Ms. Marvelous, sixth-grade English teachers. Imagine you're beginning the first day of sixth grade. I'm your principal, and, as my secret mole student observer, I'm allowing you to test out and choose which English teacher you will take this year. First up will be Ms. Marvelous, a seasoned, intuitive teacher, and expert at framing and drilling down into her parts. Then you'll visit Mr. Misery's classroom, a terrible teacher who doesn't understand parts.

## Ms. Marvelous' Class

**FIGURE 1.3** Ms. Marvelous begins class.

With a big smile, Ms. Marvelous enters her classroom, hops up on her desk, and then leans back as she crosses her legs.

MS. MARVELOUS: "Think of or look up an intriguing fun fact about an animal. Any animal. No—wait—better yet—grab a piece of paper. I want you to illustrate that fun fact quickly! I'm only giving you five minutes. I'm looking forward to seeing a detailed sketch of something amazing!"
STUDENTS: "Wait, what?" A few gasps. Perplexed looks.

MS. MARVELOUS: "I'm only kidding. Don't worry if you can't draw; scribble an animal into existence for some instant art for a quick show and tell."

…

"Time's up!"

Ms. Marvelous assigned small groups, providing them with a few loud, funny, smiling, laughing, oooo-ing, and wowing minutes of drawing. Then she calls everyone to attention, asking each student to write a sentence to describe the fun animal fact next to their illustrations, and then choose someone to share their group's most intriguing fact with the rest of the class.

You decide to draw a camel.

YOU: "Did you know camels have three eyelids?"

You share your ridiculous stick drawing of a camel with unintelligible scribbles vaguely resembling three giant drooping eyelids.

STUDENTS: Uproarious, gleeful laughter.

The other students proudly showcase other hilarious drawings, such as an elephant on a basketball court—

STUDENTS: "Elephants can't jump! That's a basketball goal right there."
"A flamingo eats with its head upside down!"

Ms. Marvelous takes over, "Do you want to know what mine is? I'll even draw it for you on the chalk board!"

Everyone watches with anticipation, giggling as Ms. Marvelous' draws a big slug with four human noses—two on its head and two on its tail.

Ms. Marvelous points to her slug.

"Slugs smell with these two." (She puts her hand on the slug's huge head noses.) "Slugs breathe with these two." (She points to its tail's smaller noses).

STUDENTS: Cracking up, smiling with wide eyes, wondering what could possibly be coming next.

Ending the activity, Ms. Marvelous exclaims, "I hope you enjoyed this. I did. Thank you all! This was so much fun, and I knew this would be an amusing way to start English comp. You all did such a fantastic job in the short amount of time I gave you!"

**FIGURE 1.4** Now she gets down to business.

MS. MARVELOUS: "Okay, now it's time to start the year with two simple words: the first word is 'to.'" (She writes "to" on the board near her slug drawing.) "The second one is 'keep.'" (She writes "keep" on the slug and continues writing …) "And I'm adding this list of words: 'suddenly,' 'thankfully,' 'sorrowfully,' 'happily,' 'boldly,' 'quickly,' 'easily,' 'continuously,' and 'carefully.'"

Then Ms. Marvelous writes a sentence, underlining three words: "Slugs have four noses *to* easily *keep* breathing."

"I want you all to write a sentence about your animal like this one. Use the words "to keep" and choose one of the other words on this list to put in the middle, then share it with your group members."

STUDENTS: [Sharing]

"Camels have three eyelids *to* <u>thankfully</u> *keep* sand out of their eyes."

"The flamingo's head goes upside down *to* <u>quickly</u> *keep* eating."

"An elephant's weight causes it *to* <u>continuously</u> *keep* standing and not jumping."

MS. MARVELOUS: "Great job! Did you know each animal sentence you created contains split infinitives? An example of a regular infinitive is 'to keep.' You split your infinitive with the word you chose to put in the middle. Generally a no-no in formal writing, the use of split infinitives sparks widespread debates. Now, take a few seconds to de-split your infinitives and share your ideas with your group on the different structures and meanings of your two animal sentences …"

When the class is over, you and the other students leave the room exhilarated, wanting to know more about split infinitives, and since you drew that camel with three eyelids, you will never forget what a split infinitive is!

## Mr. Misery's Class

You enter the classroom, taking a seat in the front row as Mr. Misery enters behind you.

**FIGURE 1.5** Mr. Misery begins lecturing.

He puts down his satchel and picks up a piece of chalk.

MR. MISERY: "Today we'll begin with split infinitives. An infinitive consists of the word 'to' and the simple form of a verb such as 'to go' and 'to read.' Can anyone give me an example of a split infinitive? Anyone?"

(No one answers.)
"An example of a split infinitive is 'to carefully assess …'" (Mr. Misery writes "To carefully assess" on the chalkboard.)

YOU: (Whispering to yourself) "Oh no. Oh no. No, no— *nooooooo.*"

He hovers, staring at the split infinitive he wrote only seconds ago before continuing his conversation with the chalkboard.
"Another example of a split infinitive is 'to quickly fix.'" (Mr. Misery writes "To quickly fix" on the board.) Then he mumbles, still looking at the board, "Can anyone add to these examples?"
Hearing no responses, he continues, "I've got another … 'To' (he writes to and says 'to' out loud) 'suddenly' (he writes

'suddenly' and says 'suddenly') 'go' (jots 'go' then says 'go')."
Next, Mr. Misery puts it all together: "To suddenly go."

"How about one more? 'To' (he writes 'to') 'sorrow-fully' (he scribbles 'sorrowfully') 'cry' (then he writes 'cry')."

Monotonal Mr. Misery's chalk touches each word, making clicking sounds for each short syllable as he reads them.

"To—sorrowfully—cry …. To-sor-row-ful-ly cry." He finally turns around to his panicked students facing the horror of being stuck in this room for an entire school year.

Then Mr. Misery dives into the heart of his lesson.

"These are all split infinitives since adverbs split the infinitives. Can anyone explain what this means? What do I mean by the word 'split?' What about the word 'infinitive?'"

You pray the bell rings soon as you try to pick your head off your desk. Then you remember your mystery novel in your bag, pull it out, and hide it on top of your textbook, but you know there's no real need to conceal it from Mr. Misery. He'd never notice.

## Marvelous or Misery?

Ms. Marvelous taught her classes similarly to Mr. Misery for many years before she understood the power and necessity of playing Framing Parts before drilling down into her lessons. However, she didn't call them parts and didn't consciously know she was playing or framing students' needs with them. She achieved this, learning the hard way how most students don't enjoy learning about English, including split infinitives. Though she knows they're only sitting there because English is a required class, she spreads the spirit of grammar many students enjoy catching after she cracked the code of exemplary teaching (what you're learning in this book). Though entirely unintentional, Mr. Misery let his students down.

For a hint of what's to come later in your training, it may surprise you that none of this classroom fun was in Ms. Marvelous' lesson plan! She had something else in mind, ready to play another much different Framing Part. She made an instant, spontaneous decision based on a signal—extreme lethargy that shouldn't exist in a classroom, especially on the first day of class! It was impossible to ignore the flashing red light signal with a blaring siren—"LETHARGY! *WARNING!* LETHARGY!"—insisting she immediately shift to an emergency frame to wake these students up and get the school year started right. Ms. Marvelous knows her parts well and knows when to change parts instinctively.

Still new to the building, let's be fair to Mr. Misery. He spent a lot of time on his split infinitives lesson plan, coming up with many examples on the board. Stuck in his content, he ignored his students and how his one-note Drilling Part impacted them. Worse, he did not frame his class, letting the dry split infinitives set the tone instead of him. Like most teachers, he didn't know he needed a frame nor that Framing Parts existed. He may never know; if he doesn't, he cannot hope to achieve teaching excellence.

It's essential to continue to stress the difference between "playing" parts and acting. Ms. Marvelous did not suddenly change who she was and become someone else as actors must do. She assumed a part involving natural actions and activities she would otherwise plan. Still, her intuition told her she needed to implement an emergency response to widespread student lethargy immediately.

Her shift required simple details such as crossing her legs and plopping herself on her desk, taking a relaxed posture to set an easy, unexpected tone. Then she spontaneously choreographed an exercise from the repertoire of stored activities from her teaching experience she knew would be fun. Mr. Misery wasn't acting either, though he was unaware that he still "played" a part.

# Part Profiles

The rest of this chapter (and the book) will feature what I consider the 12 main parts of teaching. To differentiate between the parts more clearly, I scrutinize their profile presets, in other words, the teaching tempos they establish, the volume of their voice and the noise level of the class, how and where they move, and the way they hold themselves, especially their postures. Each part brings a purpose and a vibe. Decisions on how you connect these vibes (predetermined and split-second) make the difference between a good and great teacher. Though I believe these 12 parts comprise excellent teaching, please feel free to push back and establish yours as you see fit.

## Framing Part Profiles

Again, Framing Parts help teachers establish a feeling and tone, especially valuable at the beginning and end of lessons, but also anytime, and they set up how I deliver content. My Framing Parts include:

- ◆ "The Praiser" (providing positive reinforcement)
- ◆ "The Dominator" (to establish control)

- ◆ "The Yielder" (to offer freedom and creativity)
- ◆ "The Punisher" (when it's necessary for accountability and consequences)

As should have been evident in Ms. Marvelous' example, the time it takes to play a Framing Part (setting the tone) is usually much shorter than the Drilling Part (the nitty-gritty aspects of teaching).

I detail the way I play Framing Parts over the following pages. Study my specs closely and decide if you share any of them with me (I guarantee you will!) and ways they differ from how you play them. Let's start by learning my details for when I play The Praiser.

## The Praiser

I refer to this part as my home base.

**FIGURE 1.6** "I joyously celebrate met or exceeded outcomes or behaviors."

Everybody wants to be praised, especially my students who badly want to please me, and I love frequently recognizing their efforts, reinforcing them to keep producing quality work. I give them enormous challenges, and I'm there to make them feel proud when they work hard and turn in deliverables meeting high standards. This part also comes in handy in setting up low-risk, easy, and fun activities that end with showering students with accolades to get them in the mood to dive more deeply into the material.

*Overall feeling:* Joyful exuberance.

*The Praiser thinks:* My students' success is my success! We did it together. The best part of this job is watching them grow; seeing them change is a sight to behold.

*The Praiser feels and says:*

♦ Astonishment. "Wow! Great work! I love your imagination and the vivid way you described things!"
♦ Pride. "I'm so proud of you!"
♦ Happy. "You deserve to celebrate!"
♦ Giving. "Congratulations, this gold star is for you!"
♦ Relief. "Despite the rocky start, you did it! But I knew you could do it!"

*Students feel and say:*

♦ Pride—"Hey, thank you so much for your leadership and believing in me!"
♦ Accomplishment—"That took a lot of work!"
♦ Smarter—"I feel like I know a lot more than I did."
♦ Thrilled—"I'm so excited and happy it turned out well."
♦ Ready—"I'm looking forward to the next challenge."

*What The Praiser does:*

♦ Smiles from ear to ear.
♦ Shares and rejoices over the success with the class.
♦ Exclaims pride over an individual student's success.

- ◆ Amplifies an individual student's good news with other students.
- ◆ Informs buoyed students of the next challenges coming soon.
- ◆ Sings something happy and uplifting such as "Celebration" by Kool and the Gang or "We are the Champions" by Queen (showing my age).

*The tempo The Praiser establishes:* Sometimes fast and upbeat when success is newly known, and other times a slower pace to soak in all the joy.

*How loud is The Praiser?* Loud to very loud.

*How and where does The Praiser move?*

- ◆ Jumping up and down
- ◆ "Victory arms"
- ◆ Clapping
- ◆ Running over somewhere to celebrate

*What is The Praiser's posture?* Varies—relaxed to alert, depending on the situation.

Every teacher wants to praise their students, and they love it when I play this essential Framing Part. I know I am doing an excellent job if I can play this part as often as possible!

---

### What Kind of Praiser Are You?

Think about your version of The Praiser. Do most of my specs match yours? What aspects of your teaching style are different than mine? (For instance, maybe "victory arms" isn't your style?) Take some time to think about your version of The Praiser's part presets.

What do you feel and say when you praise your students? Precisely what do your students feel and say when you play this part? What specific things do you do? How would you describe the tempo of your class when you play this part? How loud is your voice, and what's the general volume of the class when you praise? How do you hold yourself? What would be a more apt name for your "praiser part?" Please ask and answer these questions after considering the details of the rest of my parts on the following pages.

## The Yielder

Although The Praiser is my home base, my favorite Framing Part is The Yielder. I consider myself a very creative and self-motivated learner, and I love to be free to explore and do my own thing; naturally, I love to offer the same to students who crave this environment. Notably, The Yielder comes in handy for necessary surprise shifts, such as when I need to cut the apron strings and if I find myself hand holding too much. The following specs describe my version of The Yielder:

**FIGURE 1.7** "I create the freest atmosphere possible by releasing control, encouraging exploration and student ownership."

*Overall feeling:* Wide-open hopeful freedom to explore and create with less direct supervision.

*The Yielder thinks:* I am hoping the next time I see the student/s, they will present excellent work, but I'm ready for any course corrections.

*The Yielder feels and says:*

♦ Hope. "I hope you'll do great things and use the time wisely."
♦ Generous. "I'm setting aside time for you to dig into the assignment. Please let me know if you need more time to complete your thought process."
♦ Confident. "I have enough self-esteem to let them go."
♦ Grateful. "I am so glad the students seem to think for themselves."
♦ Respected. "I love this job again!"

*Students feel and say:*

♦ Trust—"All this time I've been given makes me trust the teacher."
♦ Responsible—"What I do over this time will help gain the teacher's confidence in my abilities."
♦ Creative—"My mind is bursting with ideas now that the teacher sent me out on my own to think for myself and produce quality work."
♦ Ownership—"Now that teacher sent me away, whatever comes of this is what I put into it. It's all me."
♦ Respect—"I respect the heck out of this teacher for turning me loose and letting me experience this growth!"

*What The Yielder does:*

♦ Sets up the concept of not being present with student/s much or at all.
♦ Resists the urge to pop in to check on the students' progress too frequently.
♦ Figures out how to track student deliverable time-lines and deadlines without being there physically.
♦ Prepares to potentially shift to another Framing Part to hold students accountable if they're not putting in the work; determine if yielding can continue.

*What classroom tempo does The Yielder establish?* Steady.

*How loud is The Yielder?* Regular to very loud volume (when visible).

*How and where does The Yielder move?* Variable, but soon will be nearby, or absent (so not apparently moving).

*What is The Yielder's posture?* Loose and casual.

---

### How Do You Yield?

Think about the times you yield when you teach. If your teaching is anything like mine, you'll expect to yield a few times during a lesson and, sometimes, an entire class period. Active learning requires a great deal of yielding, so understanding your version of The Yielder contributes to better student experiences and outcomes.

---

## The Dominator

My next Framing Part, The Dominator, sounds scary, but it's not; I sometimes have little control of my classroom and must shift into a dominant role to regulate order. (An alternate name might be "The Controller," but that sounds much worse to me!) I found this Framing Part essential to my teaching, especially knowing how I establish a controlled environment necessary for concentration and production. Following are more details about The Dominator, a fascinating part I play:

**FIGURE 1.8** "I step in to establish or regain control."

*Overall feeling:* Authoritarian leadership.

*The Dominator thinks:* These students haven't been introduced to this material. Or—I realize students have chosen not to meet learning (or behavioral) outcomes. I will create and implement a no-nonsense atmosphere. I command attention. I demand respect.

The Dominator feels and says:

♦ Skeptical. "They don't know this stuff yet."
♦ Pressured. "It's my responsibility to get them to learn."
♦ Secure. "I'm steering this ship exactly where it needs to go."
♦ Ready. "I'm willing to do this because it's necessary."
♦ Assured. "Knowing my teaching, I predict I won't have to dominate very long."

*Students feel and say:*

- Shocked—"What just happened?"—or—"What is about to happen?"
- Ready—"Heads up!"
- Alert—"I'm clear-eyed and wide awake."
- Eager—"The class is set up so formally; I want to make sure to stay one step ahead."
- Controlled—"Heads down, I know I just need to hold on and stay focused."

*What The Dominator does:*

- Makes sure to be visible at all times.
- Stays physically and verbally formal.

*The classroom tempo The Dominator establishes:* Marching. Consistent.

*How loud is The Dominator?* Regular-to-louder volume.
*How and where does The Dominator move in the classroom?*

- Marching wall-to-wall in the front of the classroom, stopping at each wall, the middle of the classroom, and then to the other wall.
- Steady, walking up and down and back up all the rows.
- Minimal facial animation.
- Thoughtful, if not rigid arm movements.

*What is The Dominator's posture?* Formal, stiff as a board.
My version of The Dominator evolved and strengthened over time. I found out the hard way that excellent teachers must not avoid playing this part; I didn't allow

myself to play it back in my early teaching days, and therefore wasn't taken seriously. Since my students weren't much younger than me back then, I was trying to be too much of a friend—*a big mistake!*

---

### How Do You Dominate?

Many teachers feel awkward and unnatural playing The Dominator until they realize how much it ties to excellent teaching. Are you at ease with "dominating?" How do you reign in your students? Think about and list out reasons it's necessary. How does playing this part relate to student respect? Do you think your version of The Dominator is appreciated or resented by your students? Although I contend dominating is necessary for every teacher, maybe you can think of a name that suits your part better than my straightforward "The Dominator."

---

## The Punisher

Next up is The Punisher. Like The Dominator, the name I gave this Framing Part sounds horrifying, but it cuts to the chase and is essential to successful teaching careers. It's a fact of life in teaching that you will have to provide consequences to students.

**FIGURE 1.9** "I provide necessary, reasonable, and fair consequences for unmet learning outcomes and rule-breaking behaviors."

*Overall feeling:* Disappointment and optimism.

*The Punisher thinks:* I never enjoy assigning failing grades, but here I go. I hope this student realizes how much I care about them and how much I care about the rest of the class.

*The Punisher feels and says:*

- Anxious. "I have suspicions about what could be in that stack of ungraded papers."
- Apprehensive. "I can't put off assigning this unsatisfactory grade any longer."
- Sad. "This student could have performed much better."
- Hopeful. "I will change these students' trajectories as best I can."
- Loving. "I have to do this because I care. A lot."

*Students feel and say (varies):*

- Grateful (the unpunished students)—"Since I studied so hard and got a good grade, I sure am glad this teacher cares about the integrity of the class."
- Awake—"I need to get my act together."
- Sad/Mad/Worried/Ashamed—"I can't believe that %$#^@ teacher gave me an F!"
- Vulnerable—"What will happen to me if I fail this course?"
- Frustrated—"I thought I knew that stuff."

*What The Punisher does:*

- Brings a mix of compassion, alarm, and immediacy.
- Prepares to have uncomfortable heart-to-heart conversations.

♦ Carefully details why punishment was needed.
♦ Gives frank descriptions of future consequences for continued underperformances without sugar coating.
♦ Offers help and provides action steps necessary for future success.

*The classroom tempo The Punisher establishes:* Very slow so students can understand the gravity of my consequences.
*How loud is The Punisher?* Soft to average volume.
*How and where does The Punisher move?* Situational.

When students slack:

• For a class: a formal careful, slow gate with no arm motions when moving to the spot to explain unmet outcomes.
• One-on-one: formal, cautious gate, slowly approaching a student to explain unmet outcomes.

When students tried: Much more casual strides and looser arm movements.

*What is The Punisher's posture?* Varies—relaxed to alert, depending on your knowledge (or instincts) on whether students put in the work.

Unless you're a sadist, nobody likes playing this part. It often breaks my heart. You can see how much care I put into The Punisher to be as compassionate as possible. However, teachers must be clear-eyed and realistic; sure, we want everyone to get an A, but a variety of circumstances makes this impossible in most cases.

## Watching Yourself Punish

Do you agree that playing your version of The Punisher well means ensuring fairness? How do you feel when penalizing students? How does compassion factor in for you? Do you avoid or embrace playing this part? What happens to your students when you neglect this part? How does your teaching style impact how your students view you when you punish, and do you consider your style authentic? How would you describe yourself in this part to your colleagues? Is there a better term for this role for your version of The Punisher?

Sometimes when I explain the concept of Framing Parts to new teachers, they will say something like, "I don't really understand this because what would be the part I play when I grade students' papers? And what about the part I play when I'm planning my lesson?" The easy answer: Framing Parts can only be played while in the context of teaching students to set up "the feeling," steering toward an intended direction.

Now that you know my Framing Parts, did you agree with mine? It's hard for me to imagine that any teacher would not share these basics, but I can understand how others might play more parts than I do.

## Drilling Part Profiles

Once I successfully establish "the intended feeling" with a Framing Part, I can drill down into my lesson with its subject-related content. The following Drilling Part specs include the fundamental ways I deliver content and interact with students. Do any of these parts I play seem familiar to you?

## The Coach

Sports coaches pay searing attention to the details of their athletes' performances; The Coach does the same for his students. The Coach cares a lot, and is closely watching, monitoring, and "scoring" everything. I love playing this part because it puts me in a role I cherish—being a motivator in someone's life.

**FIGURE 1.10** "I motivate and maximize my student's/s' potential through heavy encouragement and thoughtful course corrections."

*Overall feeling:* Motivational advice as if on a sports sideline.

*The Coach thinks:* I will help my students win. I will bring out the best in them, whatever their capabilities. I will be brutally honest, but they know I only have their best interest in mind.

*The Coach feels and says:*

◆ Playful. "This is going to be so much fun! And I'm having as much fun as you are!"

- ◆ Interested. "If I didn't love this subject, I wouldn't be a coach."
- ◆ Eager. "I can't wait to see what's next for you."
- ◆ Awe. "Your progress is inspiring. Keep going."
- ◆ Calm. "Consider me your rock. Take my advice, follow through, and you'll do great things."

*Students feel and say:*

- ◆ Courageous—"This teacher makes me want to take risks and grow."
- ◆ Energized—"I feel wide awake and alive right now!"
- ◆ Motivated—"The teacher makes me want to reach higher and farther."
- ◆ Strong—"I have the tools I need to succeed."
- ◆ Capable—"I've got this!"

*What The Coach does:*

- ◆ Sets incremental goals and objectives.
- ◆ Establishes long-term visions and expectations.
- ◆ Watches student's/s' work very carefully.
- ◆ Measures progress in exquisite detail.
- ◆ Provides truthful feedback.
- ◆ Speaks in a motivational tone.
- ◆ Supports students enthusiastically.

*The tempo The Coach establishes:* Variable, depending on observed progress. Sometimes slow for emphasis, other times very upbeat.

*How loud is The Coach?* Variable. Sometimes soft, other times loud, depending on motivational situations.

*How and where does The Coach move?* As an athletic coach might jump out of their seat or run up and down the field waving their arms, I am ready to move equivalently. I'll also sit contemplatively, especially in a "nail-biter" situation.

*What is The Coach's posture?* Mainly formal, upright, and ready.

Though I enjoy playing The Coach, it can be exhausting, especially if needs involve many individual students at once. However, because I've known The Coach for so long, I make careful decisions on the amount of time necessary to be effective while guarding the energy I have to give.

---

### Playing Your Coach

How do you actively motivate? What does your focused enthusiasm and positive reinforcement look, sound, and feel like to your students? How does respect factor in when you support student's/s' goals? Does patience matter in your version of The Coach? Can you think of a more appropriate name for this part?

---

## The Commentator

An intriguing and nuanced Drilling Part, The Commentator, appears when I know I need to be straight with my students, watching them closely, then providing detailed commentary on their work as if I were a narrating sportscaster, perpetually making myself clear, reminding students of instructions and rules, and then waiting to see what they choose to do. The most common scenario involves discovering whether my student/s took good advantage of the freedom to explore, create, and grow. I also play this part to provide an opportunity for redemption, a choice to bounce back from the consequences of not meeting outcomes.

**FIGURE 1.11** "I'm watching students like a sportscaster calling a game, I'm waiting to see what they will do."

*Overall feeling:* Data, rules, facts-driven.

*The Commentator thinks:* It will be interesting to see what happens now and next.

*The Commentator feels and says:*

- ◆ Hopeful. "I still expect you to succeed."
- ◆ Realistic. "I'm monitoring your current trajectory, and I hope you are determined to do well."
- ◆ Honest. "I ensure students know where they stand."
- ◆ Responsive. "I'll be happy to explain the assignment again, but it's all up to you at this point."
- ◆ Ready. "I'm prepared to shift when I know what the student chooses to do."

*Students feel and say:*

- ◆ Clear—"Teacher gave me tremendous knowledge and a strong skills foundation, and I know I'm still being offered independence to explore, create, and grow. I think I will do those things now."

◆ Thankful—"I'm under surveillance, and I can see the teacher still has a bit of confidence in me, at least at this moment. Onward and upward!"

◆ Grateful—"I'm being watched after failing my exam, and I'm grateful the teacher gave me this opportunity."

◆ Informed—"I get it now. I really do."

◆ Confused—"I don't get it at all, but will."

◆ Apathetic—"I don't get it, but I might return to it later. Well, probably not."

◆ Nothing—"." [They are no-shows.]

*What The Commentator does:*

◆ Watches.
◆ Hopes.
◆ Waits.
◆ Conspicuously offers timely reminders of assignment instructions and rubrics.
◆ Tends to the due date calendar in the background.
◆ Asks if students need clarity on any instructions.

*The tempo The Commentator establishes:* Steady.

*How loud is The Commentator?* Normal volume.

*How and where does The Commentator move?* Directly to a student, a group, or straight and steady in to teach.

*What is The Commentator's posture?* Normal when moving and formal, more rigid when "commentating."

When I play The Commentator, I feel like my personal teacher assistant—informing, watching, explaining, and waiting.

---

**How Do You Commentate?**

If you've been a teacher for a while, you know how it feels to watch and wait as you communicate clearly with your students. How does your version of this part's presets help your students understand? Think about your tempo and how it lends to student clarity. Perhaps you speak matter-of-factly as I do?

---

## The Parent

Often, students need more personal attention and compassion. Enter The Parent. This Drilling Part requires careful attention, and I must be cautious when blurring teacher and "caregiver." Yes, I care a lot, but when I play this part, I know I must draw a definitive line to save my sanity. I am not their real parents. I am not related to them at all, but they are "mine," and I know I have an enormous responsibility to be there for them; however, I am not a therapist. I am always aware of "the line," which involves trying my best to get out of this part as fast as possible while serving my student's/s' needs as best I can.

**FIGURE 1.12** "I show compassion, provide caring support, and make students feel safe while setting limits and establishing clear expectations."

*Overall feeling:* I'm here for you.

*The Parent thinks:* I see and understand my students' vulnerabilities, and they need me to listen. Since I'm not a therapist, I know I won't be able to (and don't have time and should not be expected to) provide full emotional support; still, I let my guard down, acknowledge what they are going through, helping them make better decisions. As all human beings do, students go through a lot inside and outside the classroom, and I'm often their primary point of contact. I will be aware of my student's/s' vulnerabilities and keep up with what's happening with their progress.

*The Parent feels and says:*

- ◆ Confident. "I'm in a position to help you."
- ◆ Compassion. "I know this is tough."
- ◆ Sensitive. "I understand."
- ◆ Flexible. "I can move your deadline back a few days."
- ◆ Optimistic. "I hope things improve for you."

*Students feel and say:*

- ◆ Frustrated—"I don't think I will ever understand this stuff."
- ◆ Anxious—"I'm worried I am going to fail."
- ◆ Insecure—"I may not be smart enough to succeed in this class."
- ◆ Hopeless—"I'm giving up."
- ◆ Exhausted—"Too much. It's all just too much to deal with right now."
- ◆ Thankful—"I appreciate you taking the time to give me some extra attention and care."

*What The Parent does:*

◆ Makes sure to be accessible to students.
◆ Appears approachable to students.
◆ Lends an ear and listens intently.
◆ Acknowledges understanding.
◆ Keeps an eye out for what the student isn't saying about what they're going through.
◆ Where appropriate and when needed, find outside guidance for students.
◆ Carefully gauges whether, depending on the situation, students might be better off receiving tough love.
◆ Makes sure not to let students hover with The Parent, a part that should be played very sparingly and only when necessary.

*The tempo The Parent establishes:* Very slow.
*How loud is The Parent?* Soft-spoken.
*How and where does The Parent move?* Very limited movements in a classroom and careful movements in one-on-one situations.
*What is The Parent's posture?* Casual yet assured.

Even more than The Coach, playing The Parent can be exhausting! I'll bet you're nodding hard right now. It took years to strike the necessary energy balance I'm able (or willing!) to give while offering as much empathy and compassion as possible.

## How Do You Parent?

Do you play The Parent in your practice? If so, do you agree with me on the necessary precariousness of this part? Think carefully about how you play it and how your teaching style differs from your colleagues. Do you think you overplay, underplay, or ignore this role? How do your students view you in your version of "The Parent?" What might be a better name for you?

## The Lifeguard

Trained to watch swimmers intensely but not go in the water unless necessary, The Lifeguard stands ready. For instance, if I see someone "choking," I'll hang back a bit to make sure they're "breathing," and if I detect actual danger, I'll "jump into the pool" to save them. If I jump in too soon, I might do more harm than good, interrupting a swimmer's self-recovery. It's the same in the classroom!

FIGURE 1.13 "I let students play and enjoy their creative production, but I'm continuously scanning, ready to jump in to help if needed."

*Overall feeling:* Cautious autonomy.
*The Lifeguard thinks:* I know their growth depends on being able to think for themselves. I wonder how long until the students need me?

*The Lifeguard feels and says:*

◆ Confident. "I'm just going to hang back."
◆ Interested. "I love watching students working on worthwhile projects I assigned them."
◆ Happy. "Playing The Lifeguard is one of the best aspects of teaching."
◆ Proud. "I built an active learning ecosystem, and I'm encouraged that my students choose to enthusiastically participate."
◆ Successful. "Wow! What a wonderfully creative atmosphere!"

*Students feel and say:*

◆ Fun—"I'm enjoying this assignment."
◆ Ownership—"I can explore without micromanagement."
◆ Creative—"I'm gathering new ideas I didn't think of before."
◆ Safe—"I know if I need help or have questions that the teacher is right over there."
◆ Thankful—"Woops, I screwed that one up. That's okay. I caught it on my own."

*What The Lifeguard does:*

◆ Stands back, available to students, within view, or periodically pops in and out of a classroom.
◆ If in view and hearing range of student conversations, listens, but does not interfere, even if something seems incorrect or on the wrong track. (Let them make mistakes, just don't let them "drown!")

◆ Readies to join students with questions.
◆ Answers questions, offers input, then leaves.

*The tempo The Lifeguard establishes:* None. Students develop their own tempos, which will vary depending on their assignments. For example, an individual writing assignment will have a slow tempo; a maker-space team craft studio would likely be much faster—OR—steady, marching when engaged with students.

*How loud is The Lifeguard?* Silent, then average volume.

*How and where does The Lifeguard move?* Absent (so not moving). Or from the side of the room, then to a student or group of students. Or either away to the side or exit the room.

*What is The Lifeguard's posture?* Not applicable (yielding)—average (engaged)—then not applicable (yielding again).

The Lifeguard represents excellent teaching, but it takes a lot for me to get students in a position where I can stay away "on my chair."

---

### Your Lifeguard

Every teacher plays a version of The Lifeguard. Do you share any of its details with me? How often do you play this part? Do you enjoy it? Have you recognized ways you monitor progress and milestones when keeping away? Is staying away hard for you?

---

## The Boss

Sometimes you face teaching students who misbehave, generally don't care, or refuse to complete assignments no matter what you do and how hard you try. For instance, when I have exhausted The Coach and let my guard down when playing The Parent to no avail, I'll reluctantly become

FIGURE 1.14 "I'm super organized and provide clear directives and no-nonsense, non-flexible expectations. In complete control, I have my student's/s/s' best interest in mind—their growth."

The Boss. (Thank goodness I rarely need to play this part.) Playing The Boss means the direction of my teaching is not going as well as I hoped for various reasons.

*Overall feeling:* Working in a job with a strict boss who doesn't tolerate nonsense.

*The Boss thinks:* This isn't my natural teaching style, and I don't enjoy it, but I have no choice now except to be strict in everything I do.

*The Boss feels and says:*

♦ Sure. "They don't know this stuff"—or "They are slacking off."
♦ Caution. "I have to move carefully and clearly through this lesson plan."
♦ Ready. "I'm closely checking off met milestones."
♦ Proactive. "It takes a lot to pull this off."
♦ Optimistic. "I really don't enjoy playing this part, but if I persist, I know it's likely temporary."

*Students feel and say:*

♦ Startled—(Gulp) "Wow, this teacher means business!"
♦ Alert—"I'd better pay attention so I can understand what the teacher expects of me."
♦ Expectant—"What could be coming next?"
♦ Amazed—"Dang. This teacher is strict."
♦ Valued—"I'm thankful for this structure right now."

*What The Boss does:*

♦ Creates structure.
♦ Makes it impossible to lose interest.
♦ Establishes a palpable formal vibe in the classroom, with groups and one-on-ones.
♦ Teaches from bell to bell without exception.
♦ Offers the least flexibility to student requests.

*The tempo The Boss establishes:* A consistent, driving pulse from start to finish.

*How loud is The Boss?* Regular volume. (It's already intense enough so I don't use a loud voice.)

*How and where does The Boss move in the classroom?*

♦ Marching wall-to-wall in the front of the classroom, stopping at each wall, the middle of the classroom, and then to the other wall.
♦ Steady, walking up and down and back up all the rows.
♦ Minimal facial animation.
♦ Thoughtful, if not rigid arm movements.

*What is The Boss's posture?* Formal, stiff.

Back in my lousy teaching days, I played this part a lot because I was insecure, but these days, I rarely ever need to (but I'm never afraid to).

---

### You, The Boss

In your teaching, do you sometimes need to establish total control, micromanaging and monitoring your student's/s' every move? If so, which presets do you share with me when I play The Boss? How and where do you move in this part? Which details become most important in establishing yourself as The Boss? I find one of the most important ways I keep control is by keeping my tone of voice consistent.

---

## The Friend

Sometimes students need me to be more like a friend than a teacher. The Friend requires me to let my guard down like I'm "one of them." I can only play this part when I'm confident that students are doing great work in a more hands-off setting. However, even more precarious than playing The Parent—by far—The Friend must be very sparingly played. You cannot be and are not your student's/s' actual friend(s) until they graduate. Overplaying The Friend is the surest way to lose respect. Even though I now can instinctively know when to play The Friend, I can feel myself hesitating, with my subconscious cautiously, thoughtfully making decisions on whether to play this part. Still, you can't be a great teacher without allowing yourself to play this role. The Friend specs include:

**FIGURE 1.15** "I bring myself into the student's world as If I were a student myself focused on helping them achieve."

*Overall feeling:* We're in this together.

*The Friend thinks:* Maybe they're stuck, or perhaps they're quickly running in the wrong direction; if they see I'm also a human who was once a student, I might be able to contribute positively.

*The Friend feels and says:*

- Interested. "How're things going?"
- Grounded. "We are all a part of the human race."
- Present. "Brief moments that connect people mean a lot to us."
- Belonging. "I remember what it was like to be a student."
- Connected. "Even though it's all about the students, as a teacher, I remembered I'm part of the academy, too."

*Students feel and say:*

- Seen—"That teacher noticed me in a cool way I appreciated."
- Heard—"I needed someone to listen at that exact time."

◆ Kindness—"Wow, what a 'real' person my teacher turned out to be!"
◆ Redirected—"Putting it to me in that friendly, relatable way got me going again."
◆ Dignified—"I feel like the teacher gets me now."

*What The Friend does:*

◆ Remembers that this part must be the least played.
◆ Stays on the lookout for moments where it's appropriate to connect in a friend-to-friend way.
◆ Makes sure only to play this role in the context of something learning-based.

*The tempo The Friend establishes:* A casual, "hanging out" tempo.

*How loud is The Friend?* Normal volume.

*How and where does The Friend move?* Goes wherever and with the flow.

*What is The Friend's posture?* Friendly and easygoing.

When I began teaching, I stayed locked playing The Friend with disastrous results that spiraled into an abyss of student disrespect and a complete loss of control. In one of those "closed-door meetings," my boss back then told me (verbatim and all caps necessary), "YOU'VE GOT TO STOP THIS 'I'M THEIR FRIEND' BUSINESS—*RIGHT. NOW.*"

Now I play this part with exquisite precision!

---

**You as Their Friend**

Does your teaching involve a version of The Friend? Do you agree with the need to play this part while maintaining a high level of caution and expediency?

How do your teaching tempo and posture contribute to the feeling of your student interactions? What could be a more relevant name for this part than The Friend?

## The Warner

Ugh! I shouldn't have to warn student/s of negative consequences on the horizon, but unfortunately, here I am. Playing The Warner means something is going wrong, and I have to do all I can to steer student/s in a new direction. Out loud and nudging behind the scenes, I stress that more time studying and working will be necessary and that time is running out. [I could have named this part "The Intervener."]

**FIGURE 1.16** "I sound the alarm that consequences may be coming due to unmet learning outcomes or unfortunate behavior decisions."

*Overall feeling:* Action and redirection—required immediately.

*The Warner thinks:* I've worked too hard to see them not succeed, and I want so much for them to reach learning outcomes I set. I'm sure they're not ready.

*The Warner feels and says:*

- ♦ Frustrated. "It can't have come to this!"
- ♦ Aggressive. "I need an emergency communications strategy."
- ♦ Skeptical. "Will I be able to change their direction?"
- ♦ Protective. "I want so badly for them to change directions!"
- ♦ Dedicated. "I'm going to try everything possible to make them understand how serious this is!"

*Students feel and say:*

- ♦ Acceptance—"Okay. This situation is what it is."
- ♦ Tense—"What am I going to do?"
- ♦ Worry—"There's not a lot of time, and I have lots of other commitments."
- ♦ Focused—"I will work with laser beam focus now."
- ♦ Resilient—"I'm taking this seriously and will emerge triumphant!"
- ♦ Indifferent—"I don't really care about what happens."
- ♦ Absent—"."

*What The Warner does:*

- ♦ Reminds students of deadlines.
- ♦ Makes students clearly understand the potential consequences of not meeting objectives.
- ♦ Reminds students of the significance of upcoming deliverables and stresses resilience and can-do-optimism.

*The tempo The Warner establishes:* Slow, methodical. Anything more would be too much in an already stressful environment.

*How loud is The Warner?* Variable, but too loud is counterproductive at this point.

*How and where does The Warner move?* Variable, but being cautious if fast and using arms.

*What is The Warner's posture?* Formal, more upright than usual.

By the time I'm required to play The Warner, I've done almost everything possible, giving them many chances to succeed. When I play The Warner, although I'm frankly warning, there's a background feeling of practically begging, with compassion, hoping they will suddenly rise to the occasion. Still, I know at this point, whatever direction they take, they probably chose that direction. (Even last-ditch, I can save them most of the time.)

---

### How You Warn

Think about how you make your students feel when you play your version of The Warner. Are you a loud or soft-spoken warner? Do you lean in or sit back? Does your tempo march fast, or do you take things slow?

---

## The Suggester

My leisurely and privileged Drilling Part, The Suggester, resembles a workshop where students bring me their deliverables in progress, and I provide constructive critiques. In this fun role, I revel in creativity with the students, suggesting ideas for their consideration. The most gratifying and fun part of playing The Suggester is watching them consider, then reject my suggestions!

**FIGURE 1.17** "I provide constructive feedback in a collaborative, friendly way."

*Overall feeling:* Thanks for the valuable advice!

*The Suggester thinks:* I'm an expert, and I am happy to give expert advice when asked, but sometimes I'll offer unsolicited suggestions to improve the student's/s' work.

*The Suggester feels and says:*

- ◆ Creative. "My mind overflows with ideas to help you with this assignment."
- ◆ Playful. "This is so much fun!"
- ◆ Chatty. "I love our back-and-forths on this."
- ◆ Energetic. "Helping you with this feeds my spirit!"
- ◆ Dedicated. "I'll keep thinking on that. Maybe I'll sleep on it and have more to say about it tomorrow!"

*Students feel and say:*

- ◆ Stimulated—"I appreciate you taking so much time to look at my work!"
- ◆ Encouraged—"Those suggestions kept me going, and they still do."
- ◆ Fascinated—"Your idea made me dig deeper in another related area, and I fell in love with the subject material."

- Productive—"I can't believe how much work I'm completing!"
- Responsible—"Thanks to your guidance, I'm in charge of my learning."

*What The Suggester does:*

- Evaluates works in progress and recommends the best ways to make constructive suggestions to help students improve their work; invites push-back and debate on each recommendation.
- With higher confidence established, allows students to make mistakes.
- Sets milestones for student reviews.

*The tempo The Suggester establishes:* Upbeat.
*How loud is The Suggester?* Loud.
*How and where does The Suggester move?*

- Enthusiastically bouncing from students' assignments-in-progress.
- Bright facial expressions
- Free use of arm gestures, including hands and fingers

*What is The Suggester's posture?* Upright and ready, yet fairly casual going with the vibe of the exciting conversations about the student's/s' work.

If only I could perpetually teach as The Suggester! I could if every student were highly productive, knew what they were doing, with a clear direction on where they were headed (not reality!). Great teachers embrace all their Drilling Parts, serving student's/s' needs, not hovering in parts they find easy and fun.

> ### How Do You Suggest?
>
> Does it feel formal or relaxed when you offer suggestions to your students? Do you primarily critique sitting down or moving around? Do you gesture? What about the tempo you establish? How would the students describe the tone of their experience when you give them feedback?

## My Part Specs, Your Part Specs

The 12 parts I explained above describe the specs of *my* parts. I gathered and defined these through visualizing my teaching. I know most teachers will be familiar with all these parts, but how you play them will be different from how I do. *Great!* You will also identify more parts. Every teacher is different.

The rest of the chapter shows you how I manage my parts with a "baked and ready" model (mine). In digesting these concepts, I recommend working with my parts and my system, then modifying mine or building your own.

## The Parts Wheel

Each part sits in a particular place that explains their relationships as visualized on the "Parts Wheel." Immediately adjacent parts contribute similar classroom tones and experiences because they address complementary student needs. Take some time to study the parts' locations on this wheel; it's crucial.

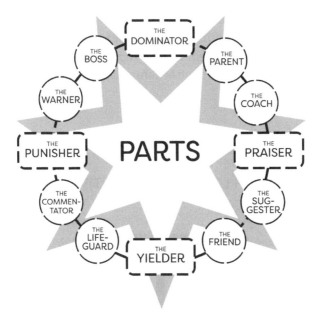

**FIGURE 1.18** The Parts Wheel

## Student Needs Quads

Notice the locations between Framing Parts, creating "Student Needs Quads." Understanding this diagram sets the foundation for automatic, reflexive changes you must make many times during a lesson or a one-on-one student interaction. Categorizing the area between the Framing Parts helps keep track of the situational parts you play. For instance, when your students need MOTIVATION, you should play The Praiser or The Dominator to set the situation, depending on their specific needs. When your students need FREEDOM, jump into The Praiser or The Yielder parts. When they need HOPE, initiate The Yielder and sometimes (surprisingly and ironically) The Punisher. And when students need TOUGH LOVE, assume The Dominator or The Punisher.

The simple diagram below represents how and why the main parts of excellent teaching fit together.

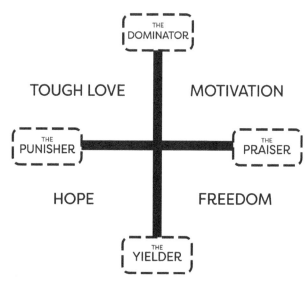

**FIGURE 1.19** Student Needs Quads

# The Trust Wheel

A hallmark of excellent teaching involves measuring the variable and changing trust levels you have for your student/s. Here, having high trust means believing they are able and willing to achieve learning or behavioral outcomes. Though implementing lessons in this book will grow your student's/s' trust they have *in you* (a primary goal for any educator hoping to become exemplary), learning to accurately monitor the shifting levels of trust you have *in them* helps you decide which part you should play.

The "Trust Wheel" displays how playing the 12 parts relates to trust. Please take a few minutes to contemplate these trust-part relationships. Do you agree? Why or why not?

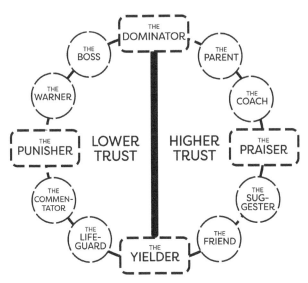

**FIGURE 1.20** The Trust Wheel

**Trust?**

Feel free to use "confidence" (or any other term that works better for you) instead of trust. Do you have confidence your students can do the work right now? Are you confident they'll meet your benchmark learning outcomes this week? Are you sure they have the will or ability to finish (or even start) a project or assignment? Here, "trust" isn't personal (there's no need to debate whether trust should be earned or granted). Whichever term you employ, excellent teaching requires the ability to know which parts you should play to position your student/s to improve or excel.

## The Presence Wheel

The "Presence Wheel" tells me how much I should be with my students.

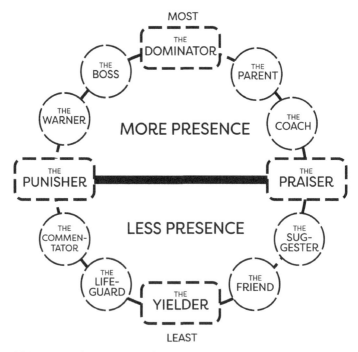

**FIGURE 1.21** The Presence Wheel

## To Be or Not to Be … There?

Do you grasp how you make decisions for engaging and disengaging with your students in the classroom, especially when doing one or the other can affect your lesson plan? Teachers who develop a knack for knowing when to pull them close and when to step away embody excellence.

# Framing Part Decisions

Remember, Framing Parts set the general feeling and tone for your teaching. Framing choices feel simple because they're clear-cut and depend on what's happening with student/s and what they need. The most foundational framing choice: will you play The Praiser or The Punisher?

**FIGURE 1.22** The most basic choice to begin a lesson

Excellent teachers rarely need to frame as The Punisher at the beginning (or end) of a lesson unless something drastic calls for it. Still, you should be ready to redirect into this part any time, whether in the middle of teaching a class, working with a team, or one-on-one with an individual student. (But we all know it's always best to frame as The Praiser.)

The second framing decision requires choosing between The Yielder and The Dominator. This choice should be quick and easy, depending on the need.

**FIGURE 1.23** The second framing decision

---

### How Do You Begin Framing?

Think about how you decide to set the tone to begin a new class period or make shifts in lessons. Do you have a go-to frame like my desire to start with The Praiser? Try to explain your thought process.

# Drilling Part Decisions

Situational decisions to play Drilling Parts depend on which Framing Part you decide to launch. As you'll soon find out in Chapters 2 and 3, knowing the details and differences between Drilling Parts increases your agility since you may play any of them at any time. Become acquainted with the apparent discrepancies when playing "opposite part pairs," the two parts located diagonally on The Parts Wheel (page 64). For example, when I play any Drilling Part, I recognize the opposite Drilling Part on the other side of the wheel's situational relationships, but I decide to play one or the other based on the student/s needs.

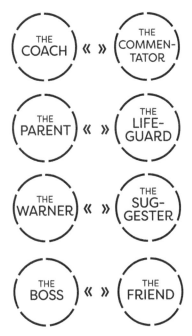

**FIGURE 1.24** Opposite Drilling Parts

---

### Your Parts Distinctions

You shouldn't expect to realize nuanced differences in playing the 12 essential parts since you're only beginning your teaching visualization journey. Don't worry! Step through the book and complete the exercises and you will quickly become very familiar with how you play your parts in big and little ways.

---

# How to Self-Observe Your Teaching

Now that you know the 12 parts, it's time to focus on your teaching, understanding the remarkable ways you play them. Every teacher brings unique styles to their classrooms. Get ready to begin watching yourself teach in your mind, identifying and describing your parts.

## Step 1: Prepare to Visualize

A bit of preparation makes the process easier. Find a comfortable space where you feel most relaxed yet able to focus. Take the time necessary for the tremendous growth coming your way by believing imagination is simple and fun; don't overthink anything. Get ready to "be there" and feel like you're actually teaching, aware of your senses. During and after observing yourself playing different parts, take quality notes and reflect on each experience.

## Step 2: Review Example Teaching Storyline Prompts

At once, read through each of the following 50 teaching situations and circumstances for one-on-one mentoring, group work, and entire classrooms before you begin visualizing to understand what's coming, allowing your mind to marinate ideas.

## Step 3: Visualize Yourself Teaching in Each Scenario

Decide which Framing Part you will play for all 50 scenario prompts to set "the feeling" and expectations for your teaching; then choose Drilling Parts to imagine how you will teach assignments and activities:

> The Praiser sets up Motivation or Freedom. [Framing Part]
>
> - Then play The Coach or The Parent if you want to motivate. [Drilling Parts]
> - Or play The Suggester or The Friend if you're going to free them to create and explore. [Drilling Parts]
>
> The Yielder brings freedom and hope for self-directed creativity and exploration. [Framing Part]
>
> - Then play The Suggester or The Friend if establishing Freedom. [Drilling Parts]
> - Or play The Lifeguard or The Commentator if establishing Hope. [Drilling Parts]

The Dominator provides motivation and tough love. [Framing Part]

- Then play The Parent or The Coach if the student needs motivation. [Drilling Parts]
- Or play The Boss or The Warner for close supervision and establishing control. [Drilling Parts]

The Punisher gives tough love, but also hope and fairness. [Framing Part]

- Then play The Warner or The Boss if continued tight control is needed. [Drilling Parts]
- Or play The Commentator for a bit of reflective redemption. [Drilling Parts]

Imagine yourself situated in your physical teaching environment. Look around. What do you see? Who do you see? What do you hear? Notice textures. What do you smell? Put yourself there!

- ◆ In detail, describe what's happening with your student/s.
- ◆ How are student/s viewing you? What's important or unimportant about how they view you right now?
- ◆ What do you know is happening? What may be bubbling under the surface? What might happen soon? How do you know? What could derail the experience?
- ◆ Focus on what you're doing and how you react and respond to everything. (Again—take notes!)
- ◆ What are you thinking?
- ◆ What are you feeling and saying?
- ◆ What are your students feeling and saying?

- How would you describe the tempo of your student/s interaction/s?
- What is the volume of your interaction/s? (How loud are you, and (if relevant) how loud is the classroom?)
- If you are moving, how? To and from where? And why?
- Describe your posture.
- How would you describe the overall feeling of this interaction?
- In a few sentences, how would you summarize this teaching experience?

---

### Example Self-Observation

Successful self-observation requires developing rich, honest teaching scenes in your imagination, but I realize starting this process is easier said than done. "Watch" me teach from this prompt:

"Overwhelmed by the material, the class seems to be giving up."

**FIGURE 1.25** My framing begins as The Yielder.

---

0:01: *Me:* Standing in front of my desk in the center of the room, I begin the hour-long class period, "Good morning, everyone! Today, I'm letting you take responsibility for your learning with team projects. I want you to work together to make a summary list of the most important takeaways you learned during the last two weeks. Please count off one to four to establish the teams."

0:04: *Students:* [Counting, otherwise silent. Staring. A few grumbling. Sliding desks together to form the team workspaces and begin talking about their assignment.]

0:05: *Me:* Handing out poster boards and big markers to each group, announcing, "In large print, please write at least ten main takeaways on the poster board. At the end of class, please hang them on the wall, and we will review them tomorrow in our next class. Don't wait on me for any more instructions. Get to work immediately."

**FIGURE 1.26** I start drilling as The Lifeguard.

0:10: I see teams of four students huddled together with their desks pointing at each other in formations that resemble starbursts. I decide to catch up on my grading as they work.

0:40: Still grading at my desk, I have been trusting each team to complete their assignments without closely monitoring their progress. I *hear* a soft din of conversations—too weak for real productivity, and I *notice* the flat smoothness of the bright white poster boards and *smell* the unmistakable fumes from all the big black permanent markers most students are holding but not using. *I peek* at the posterboards and *see a few scribbles* on one board and *nothing* on the other three.

*What's happening with my students?* Their faces seem blank and disengaged, even though I thought this activity would be valuable and fun. One team appears to be led by self-appointed facilitators, trying to pose questions and spark conversations. Still, the other three seem to have given up, fidgeting and shuffling books and papers into their bookbags in anticipation of the bell that won't ring for another 15 minutes. Junie is coming up to ask me a question.

JUNIE: "Hi, I've been sitting there with my group and they are talking about other stuff than this assignment. We are definitely not going to finish."

ME: [Flabbergasted, I wonder how I could have let this disaster of an activity happen.]
"Thanks for your honesty, Junie."

*How are the students viewing me?* I'm confident that every student in today's class considers me a time-waster-busywork-maker and resents the experience. A female student's expression and body language combine to say, "Teacher, you completely let me down today," forever etched in my mind. *The way they see* me is meaningful because I never want this to happen again!

*Under the surface*, they are daydreaming and couldn't care less about this exercise, and, *happening soon*, since it's far too late to save this activity, they will leave their nearly blank posterboards behind. I'd describe *the tempo of today's class* as slow with a surprisingly quiet volume. *My movements* were disjointed and incongruent, with no thought to my *posture*. *I think* I don't blame the students for not engaging if they weren't adequately shown how I wanted them to engage. *I'm feeling amazed* because my time going to the trouble to find posterboards for his activity did not produce the expected results.

0:59: *I'm doing and saying*, "Bye," and "Have a good next class and rest of your day," as I stand beside the door addressing students exiting the room. The *overall feeling of this class* was barely going through the motions-style boredom.

This lesson didn't go as I would have hoped (and I shouldn't have been grading papers!). It seemed as though I was overly critical, I didn't judge; I was honestly watching and describing a derailment. (Did you notice my almost nonexistent weak framing as The Yielder! I also neglected to frame the ending, a huge mistake! I just told them "goodbye.")

The Yielder I play now doesn't start by saying, "Okay, go ahead and count off and let's make some groups;" that's not a great way of establishing "a feeling" before sending them to work! These days, I consider my trove of possibilities in getting students excited about an activity before I turn them loose. Playing The Lifeguard today, my in-class activities flow smoothly because years of concentrated experience from visualizing and actual teaching fuel my intuition for monitoring timing and student's/s' progress. So, commit to "watching" yourself teach as you teach without qualifying anything. Just. Observe.

Also, please remember that I provided this more structured, time-stamped written self-observation example only to clarify the thought process; you should not worry about over-structuring your imagination! Let your mind do the work! Please take the time and energy needed to watch yourself teach in all 50 of the following scenarios, building out as many details as possible.

---

## 50 Teaching Prompts for Self-Observing

Follow the directions and begin your journey:

1. Overwhelmed by the material, the class seems to be giving up. [Above, I provide an example of teaching this scenario. Now do you.]
2. A struggling student achieves a breakthrough in their writing.
3. Brains are exhausted as one of the most intense weeks of multiple deadlines and exams comes to a close.
4. Obviously distracting the class and their productivity, the students anticipate the start of a beloved school festival.
5. Clearly suffering mental stress from a close family member's death, a student tries to hold themselves together.
6. The class is far too relaxed, too casual for the lesson's serious content.
7. A student is physically exhausted from working the late shift at the fast-food joint and can't seem to cope.

8. You announce you're letting the class out early today.
9. The entire class seems irritated by something, but you don't know what.
10. A group of students makes something exceptionally creative.
11. Someone is scared.
12. One of the teams is flying through the assignment and will be finished long before the others.
13. Liang feels inferior because they always get cut off, never getting a chance to speak in class.
14. Everyone, but especially Bob, is just staring a hole through me.
15. Meeting the challenge head-on, the class receives the highest achievement test scores in the building.
16. Your class seems manic, and mania will not work today.
17. Mindy feels anxious about an upcoming essay.
18. You witness a team losing their confidence.
19. A team experiences something exciting.
20. It's been a long day, and many students seem restless.
21. The class is losing interest.
22. Oliver uncovers something fascinating and can't wait to share it with you and later with the rest of the class.
23. You handed out failing grades to several angry students.
24. Some students in the back sleep through your lecture.
25. You caught Gabriel Hugo cheating.

26. Sitting in the front seat, loud and sarcastic Rohan ruins your lesson's flow.
27. Nima turned in terrible quality work; they've checked out.
28. Your class experienced an unsettling surprise.
29. You detect Margot's hope for getting into her first-choice college.
30. You see boredom in too many eyes during your lecture.
31. Realizing the gravity of your topic, a project team reacts in a spontaneous, serious discussion.
32. Nobody's answering your open-ended question.
33. Overtly cynical about what you're teaching, Emily shows off in front of the class.
34. Your class experiences shared joy over your announcement of a sure-to-be memorable field trip.
35. Seemingly helpless, Kai cannot understand the material no matter how many ways I explain it or how long I spend with him.
36. Ray shows optimism for a new project you assigned.
37. Students are goofing off and having inopportune fun as you try to begin your lecture.
38. Too many students act confused by your assignment's instructions.
39. A few students show profound disrespect for Moana during a class discussion.
40. Your "pair-share" (small groups of two students discuss a topic, then everyone shares what they discussed with the rest of the class) seems forced.

41. Uma gains power in student government, overtly bullying several students, most of whom have no power at all.
42. You don't know why but "profoundly depressed" describes the classroom vibe.
43. An inexperienced team working on a complex project comes to you for advice.
44. You sense Naomi's deep apathy as you teach.
45. Irresponsible Blaze awaits my approach, wide-eyed.
46. Students seem mentally stimulated.
47. Glenda looks like she feels isolated.
48. Everyone found out a student in the class was involved in a terrible accident last night.
49. Students are physically uncomfortable due to the boiler room's malfunction.
50. The principal shows up in your class to recognize Tim's significant achievement, and everyone bursts with pride.

### Spoiler alert!

Many of the 50 situational prompts included flows and signals, covered in Chapter 2—it's impossible to discuss parts without flows and signals! You'll gain experience understanding your flows and responding to signals soon.

# Parts Recap

On your way to becoming an exemplary teacher, now you know what a part is and the difference between Framing

Parts and Drilling Parts. I provided scenarios to help you understand, using examples from Ms. Marvelous and Mr. Misery, learning how parts work in practice. I explained how I identified 12 main parts that teachers play and invited you to play them. I showed you how I built out part profiles for my teaching and to adopt them as your own or modify them, suggesting you add more, eliminate any, and rename them to describe the ways you teach. Then I showed you diagrams that helped organize all the parts and the significance of their locations on the Parts Wheel. You pondered the Student Needs Quad diagram, the Trust Wheel, the Presence Wheel, how to make decisions on framing and how to think about Opposite Parts. Taking the time and effort to self-observe through the 50 scenario prompts, I trust you now have a nice list of summaries and names for your Framing and Drilling Parts. Keep going! Next, we'll spotlight flows and signals.

# 2

# Know Your Flows, Then Spot the Signals (and Practice Responding to Dozens)

> The flows you manage and the signal response system you deploy distinguish you from all other teachers on Earth.

This chapter steps you through the flows and signals relationship, showing teachers how to become intuitive. It explains how your flows create an overall student experience resulting from instinctive decisions teachers make for which parts to play and how this helps determine your unique teaching style. It also details how signals constantly appear, pushing, pulling, supporting, or potentially derailing your lesson plans, and how to develop an instinct for

DOI: 10.4324/9781003360230-3

scanning, interpreting, and knowing when or if to modify or abandon a part, decide which to play next, and how these choices affect your flows.

**FIGURE 2.1** Flows

Flows connect parts.

**FIGURE 2.2** A flow connecting two parts

Your flows matter because they help create an overall student experience that depends on the decisions you make for which parts to play, and the combination of those choices makes you "you" as a teacher, defining your unique teaching style. Sometimes I sense when my flows feel seamless. Other times I recognize when I chose a flow that didn't string my parts together effectively. You already got a feel for flows when you visualized the 50 scenarios from Chapter 1, and you'll reinforce your skills when you study my flow diagrams in this chapter. As you explore, and with your parts identified, defined, and named, think about your teaching flows. I'll step you through understanding how decisions for connecting your parts contribute to exemplary (and terrible) teaching.

## "A Flow" and "Being in a Flow State"

A flow (a noun) describes a link between parts you play when you teach, different from the prepositional phrase, "in flow" (or "in a mental state of flow") or, as some say, being "in the zone." For educators, being "in flow" directly relates to the flows we choose to connect our parts.

Hungarian Psychologist Mihalyi Csikszentmihalyi, a University of Chicago psychology professor and researcher, studied flow theory, authoring *Finding Flow: The Psychology of Engagement with Everyday Life* (1997). His book created a framework to visualize flow as a mental state depending on a challenge level and skill level variables:

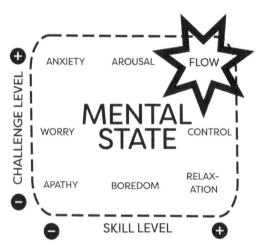

**FIGURE 2.3** Modified Csikszentmihalyi's Flow Model (p. 37)

Notice flow requires working within high challenge levels (Can you imagine a higher challenge than teaching?) and high skill levels. Waks's study of educational intuition from Chapter 1 relates to Csikszentmihalyi's model. Waks stressed how experienced teachers rapidly and unconsciously scan and connect opportunities in their classrooms. Teachers in training or just beginning will not have the skills necessary to hope to achieve "teaching flow" since, as Waks would point out, they haven't gathered enough "concentrated experience."

Teachers can gain concentrated experience in their building or campus classrooms over many years and decades. They can also decide to expedite this process by accumulating more teaching experience with serious self-observation and drawing their teaching. For me, a big part of achieving and maintaining *flow* (noun; getting in "the zone") happened because I made it a practice to intensely observe and understand my teaching *flows* (plural, the collective connections I make between the parts I play when I teach), and I was surprised how fast my skill level increased.

A legendary in-the-zone example for people in my generation features one of basketball's greatest players, Michael Jordan. Jordan scored six three-point shots in the first half of a 1992 NBA finals game, known by my friends as "the shrug game." As a young man watching that game, I remember Jordan shrugging to the camera as if, "I have no idea how I am doing this!" Jordan's high skill level of concentrated experience created his state of flow connecting the parts he played on the court: "Okay, now I'm dribbling. [The Dribbler] ➜ And now I'm setting up to shoot a three-pointer. [The Shooter] ➜ Then I hit it and watch it swoosh the net. [The Watcher] ➜ Then I smile and run down the court and shrug [The Shrugger], ➜ and now

I'm dribbling again ➤." Though overly simplified, and he wouldn't have described it like that, Mr. Jordan's state of flow directly resulted from instantaneous decisions he made based on his concentrated experience in connecting the parts he played on the court, his flows.

I'm certainly no Michael Jordan, but I contend that my mind clicked once I comprehended my flows. It didn't take long for me to achieve moments of flow, and, through self-observation and understanding "my flows" over the years, more than not, I found myself deeply in the zone/in flow most times I taught. You can achieve this, too.

It's reasonable to believe that teachers who achieve flow first can help their students do the same. However, reaching a flow state means having the skills necessary to do so: imagining and "watching" yourself teach and paying close attention to how you connect your parts quickly, required to reach and maintain your teaching flow. Keep up with the rest of the book's prompts, and I'll get you there, too.

---

### How Do "Your Flows" Put You "In Flow"?

Think of a time when you caught yourself feeling fantastic when you were teaching. Try to describe that feeling! It's wonderful! You knew you were in the zone of your most effective teaching. Though you weren't aware of flows as presented in this book, can you identify any connections between the parts you played and why they caused you to teach "in the zone?" Knowing the relationship between your flows and your reaching "flow" means you have a bright future in your building or campus!

# Signals Constantly Appear

Signals pop up, pushing, pulling, assisting, or potentially derailing your lesson plan. Great teachers know how (or whether) to respond to these indicators suggesting flows need to shift. I'll teach you how to sense and see signals and offer tips for interpreting them, taking action, or waving them off, requiring only slightly tweaking your flow or dramatically diverting to some other better or needed teaching strategy. Over time, you will develop an instinct for how, when, and why to modify or abandon a part currently being played, decide which part to play next, predict how it affects existing flows, and create new ones—*reflexively*.

**FIGURE 2.4** A signal

# Scanning for Signals

Tweaking and diverting your flows means juggling knowns and unknowns. The knowns are easy. We generally know the subject we're teaching well enough to share it with students. We're familiar with the physical classroom space, including its opportunities and limitations. We know the tools we use to teach effectively and the methods we choose to manage time to carry out our lesson plans, and we are aware of where our students are in their educational journey, whether the same or mixed.

The best teachers continuously and instinctively detect changes. They understand and tap into classroom frequencies, "feeling" the shifts and understanding their differences, the essence of educational intuition. Mystical in some ways, inventorying the "known unknowns" in your self-observations and visualizing them in diagrams can help you harness your intuition, taking out a lot of the mystery.

# Spotting and Interpreting Signals

The range of human emotions and situations pop up, bombard, and many hide. Identifying signals and making meaning of them requires practice, as does getting to know how you reply to them. Some will require strong responses, and you might decide to ignore others. Before I take you any further, understanding your treatment of signals must come first since signals shift your flows.

Follow each prompt below and self-observe your interpretation of how or if you answer these signals. Use each to imagine specific scenarios in your teaching vividly and expand them. How do you react? What do you say? What do you do? Did your tempo shift? Describe your speaking volume and the volume of the classroom. Did you feel compelled to move faster or slower? Did you travel? How are you holding yourself? What are the students thinking and feeling? How do they perceive you? Explain "the feeling" of the experience you're managing for each signal.

Following are some standard signals you can use for your teaching observation. Visualize them now!

*Optimism!* You worry your lecture may be ineffective, but then a feeling of sudden buoyancy and confidence overtakes the room as your students suddenly and strongly react.

*Irresponsibility:* You didn't realize until just now, but many students are faking being busy but behaving irresponsibly, wasting their time now and yours later with all the extra time it will take to scrutinize their thrown-together work.

*Physical exhaustion:* Delivering your lesson, you know they're paying attention, but many of your students recline back in their seats with stretched-out legs; some even slump over their desks.

*Fascination:* In a one-on-one conversation on today's material, something you say transfixes a student's attention; they want to know more.

*Panic:* You split the class into teams. One team isolated itself from the others, and you sense its members are scrambling; they do not have the skills necessary to complete the presentation exercise.

*Overwhelm:* Your mentor group session seems normal, but one student said something that shouted, "Inundation! We entirely feel stressed out."

*Hope needed:* In a flash of revelation, you discover your material is too much for many to comprehend.

*Hope appears:* You realize your students move past an important learning benchmark.

*Hope underneath*: During the facilitation of an active learning exercise, you notice a significant learning breakthrough the students can't detect yet.

*Something suddenly feels important:* As you explain the topic, one of the details rises to prominence.

*Joy!* You receive a surprise knock on the door—it's the jubilant principal with news everyone has been waiting to hear.

*Hello, anger!* You hand back a paper marked with an F grade to a smiling student, but their fury emanates.

*Shame:* You sense they feel humiliated for not meeting my expectations.

*A cry for fun:* The students would benefit from a suddenly playful activity.

*Whoa, apathy!* It seems students don't care at all about what I'm presenting!

*It's time to play:* Your tone is far too serious right now, negatively impacting the learning atmosphere.

*Sudden awareness:* It seemed as if every student in your class finally "got it" simultaneously.

*More challenge, please!* You had the idea that your material was stimulating and rigorous, but you see you were wrong.

*Boredom:* Although lost in the bliss you have for the subject you've always loved to teach, they don't feel bliss at all.

*More! More!* You can sense they don't want you to stop.

*Less! Less!* Your little voice tells you they're desperately begging you to stop.

*A new space:* Although everyone knew it was coming, the move to the temporary trailer classroom makes your teaching suddenly seem "off."

*Everything's way too casual:* Though you thought you were choreographing a serious learning activity, they see it as informal and carefree.

*Oh, no… they're confused:* Their eyes say it all, though you thought you couldn't be more precise.

*Cynicism:* The students seem to be sneering at what you're telling them, and it's getting worse.

*Disrespect:* Although it first appeared that one of your students didn't seem impressed with your suggestion, you realize blatant contempt.

*Wrong tempo:* The pace of your teaching isn't congruent with your material; your students notice.

*Thankful:* You're detecting widespread gratitude.

*Lack of confidence:* The class seems to shrink as you provide them with frank, constructive criticism.

*Helplessness:* You realize a student you've been coaching has stopped trying.

*Waning interest:* The energy you sustain until now vanishes from the room.

*Depression:* You detect a will to learn, but something's extinguishing their fire and deteriorating their focus.

*Inferiority:* You know imposter syndrome when you see and feel it.

*Restlessness:* You didn't notice until now, but they are fidgeting.

*Sarcasm!* A student responds over and over to my questions with utter disdain.

*Sleepiness:* You suddenly notice many heads bobbing, eyes closing.

*Impatience:* You can't delay a minute longer.

*Trust lost!* As you lead a class discussion, you realize few (maybe zero) students read any part of the assignment.

*Covert anxiety:* Without visible clues, you discern widespread student trepidation over the upcoming exam.

*Overt anxiety:* They're telling you about their exam apprehension.

*Irritation:* As you review the calendar of deadlines, you catch a glimpse of a few eye rolls and a lot of grimaces.

*Mania:* Something is making the students extremely jumpy!

*Physical discomfort*: The boiler room stopped working this morning, and you can see teeth clattering.

*Too straightforward*: You realize the content you deliver is dry as toast.

*Excitement.* When you stop talking and look back at your students, it seems like they're about to burst!

---

### Your Signals and Your Teaching Brand

It's fun to take on signals, isn't it?

Do you realize how "signal interpretation diversity" is such a beautiful thing? You interpret and respond to signals differently than all other teachers. Embrace how you uniquely decide to answer or ignore signals as a significant contributor to your particular brand of teaching.

---

You assuredly changed parts many times to visualize how you responded to the various signals. Please look closely at your decisions for why, how, and when to change parts.

## Flows and Signals Details

The following pages describe how I see flows and signals in greater detail. I believe teachers can benefit from realizing the complexity of these decisions; however, I also stress not bogging yourself down with these details for too long! Seeing this once will turn a switch on that can never be turned off and therefore doesn't require overstudying.

Doodling teaching scenarios on my whiteboard when I began visualizing my teaching, I enjoyed a freestyle, not "paint-by-numbers" experience, and I want the same for you! So, when you work through the next section, please realize these details must not be part of any script you bring into your class and shouldn't be considered step-by-step directives! I'm simply sharing the bits in my thought process in defining my teaching. Take some time and decide if you recognize similarities and differences in your practice. Then move on; let your "on switch" work for you to solidify your understanding of how you teach by absorbing, not overthinking.

## Adjacent Parts' Flows

Neighboring flows feel like logical connections on the Parts Wheel, addressing predictable situations and circumstances. They seem natural because I'm anticipating providing a logical next need. For instance, playing The Coach I figure I'll soon need to offer extra support as The Parent or frame celebration for meeting an outcome as The Praiser.

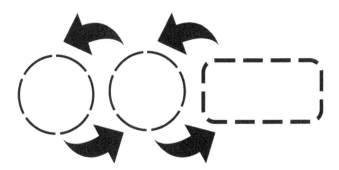

**FIGURE 2.5** Adjacent Parts Flows

## Adjacent Parts Signals

Sometimes signals remind me to remain in the part I'm playing for a while before connecting to an adjacent part. Suppose I'm ending my class period playing The Parent. I'm readying to frame as The Dominator before sending the students out the door. What if we suddenly learned upsetting news that has nothing to do with the class but affected everyone during the lesson? I'll assuredly confront the terrible news, taking extra time to keep playing The Parent for a bit longer, acknowledging the bad news with compassion and empathy, then end with a gentler (but still in control) dominator frame. Other teachers may choose to ignore this signal and end the class since it is nearly over.

**FIGURE 2.6** Adjacent parts' signal choices

### Would you Have Heeded the "Terrible News" Signal?"

Would you have stayed in The Parent part longer to acknowledge the upsetting news, stealing a few extra minutes to recognize the cloud hanging heavy?

## Quad Flows

Quad Flows are big picture flows. Quads help address primary student needs, and they're anchored by my four Framing Parts. Thinking in Quads allows me to pinpoint flow nuances required in effective teaching. These nuances depend on the different perspectives driven by "inflows" and "outflows." (Stay with me here; a basic understanding of Quad Flows makes the difference between "great" and "best" teachers.)

Depending on how I frame my teaching, my perspectives will differ when I play parts in, for instance, the Motivation Quad featured in Figure 2.7.

Notice the shape of the arrow starting at The Praiser at point "A" and ending at The Dominator (point "B"). At these points, my perspectives are very different when I need to set a tone.

For instance, if I'm framing as The Dominator (see the star with the "A"), this flow includes past decisions on those two parts I recently played (notice the white-shaded parts inside the black arrow) required a needed shift in my tone. Maybe I'm teaching a classroom of students just off a celebration of a met learning outcome. (See how I began this flow framing as The Praiser and moved toward The Dominator?) I drilled "up" through the Motivation Quad. Notice how I taught as The Coach and I shifted up to The Parent (my students must have become needy). Continuing through the flow, I reset "the feeling" currently being provided by The Praiser to the one I'll create as The Dominator because something happened that required me to assume new control, driving a different classroom tone.

Conversely, suppose I'm framing in this same Motivation Quad flow as The Praiser (flowing up from the star with the "B"). In that case, I'm sending the class off to let The Coach do his thing, and I'm hoping he'll send the student/s back to The Praiser to reframe great news, then I'll decide where to go from there, but it's possible The Dominator takes over instead.

I realize the tongue-twister aspect of trying to explain these made-from-my-mind definitions. However, this section may be the essential part of this book. Understanding the Quad Flows fundamentals becomes vital to understanding hemisphere flows, next and also crucial.

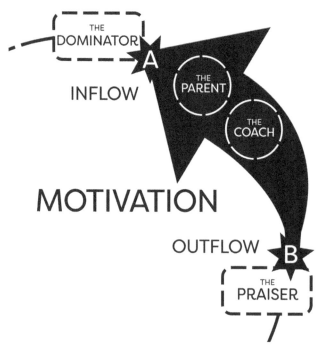

**FIGURE 2.7** Quad inflows and outflows

# Hemisphere Flows

Combining two adjacent Quads, hemisphere flows help me meet compound student needs. When I play a part in any Quad, I anticipate potential future parts I'll play that make the best "flow sense," usually located in adjacent Quads. For instance:

> *Right hemisphere/Motivation and Freedom Quad flows* require shifting between hands-on, often one-on-one, interactive, inspiring, and encouraging parts. This hemisphere requires mental and physical agility to know when to bring them in and let go. It also means I'll play parts where I step back and let them take risks, try new things independently, and trust in their capabilities.
>
> *Bottom hemisphere/Hope and Freedom Quad flows* generally feel like I'm teaching a lab of experimental trial and error in a creative setting where I stand back. This hemisphere requires tremendous background logistics to play each part successfully.
>
> *Top hemisphere/Tough Love and Motivation Quad* flows mean I'm back-and-forth between inspirational mentoring and necessary micromanagement.
>
> *Left hemisphere/Tough Love and Hope Quad flows* combine close supervision and required structure with opportunities for reflecting and developing strategies to get back on track.

---

### An Easy Way to Understand Flows

Imagining student/s moving toward and away from you provides a great way to think about and understand flows, particularly hemisphere flows. For instance, imagine you are standing still and watching a student coming toward you. They have needs, and once they arrive, you'll begin playing a part required to support them in meeting expectations and outcomes. After helping, you'll send the student to another parts player, ready to provide different needs, watching them "flow away."

---

## Motivation and Freedom Flows: The Praiser's Perspective

Varied, challenging, engaging right hemisphere flows feature parts that make up (what I consider) the fun teaching hemisphere. Moving in or away from The Praiser provides me many growth opportunities and fun because I get to dip in and out of the assortment of teaching scenarios: sometimes very engaged as The Coach and enjoying teaching as The Suggester. The Friend and The Parent live in this hemisphere, and I must play these complex parts with concern and care. These two parts provide dynamism to my teaching when precisely applied. If I can keep students on this side of the wheel, the students and I will love the experience.

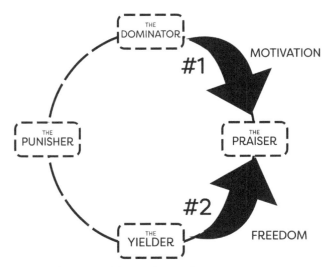

**FIGURE 2.8** The Praiser's hemisphere inflows

*I'm giving lots of humanness, and I'm here and all in with you! (#1)* I'm putting my all into close-contact teaching because my being there makes a big difference, improving their work. Because I'm close by, I know how to motivate them to improve continuously, and I can see the improvement happening in real time. Standard signals include optimism, awareness, thankfulness, physical exhaustion, overt anxiety, and underlying anxiety.

*I'm enjoying popping into your projects. (#2)* In an ideal, symbiotic relationship with The Yielder, who sets the tone for creative exploration, we combine my positive reinforcement and his active learning ecosystem along the Parts Wheel. It feels like I'm working *with* my students, and I hope we will continue to share ideas and make improvements. Common signals include joy, fascination, optimism, thankfulness, excitement, overt anxiety, underlying anxiety, and, sometimes, irresponsibility.

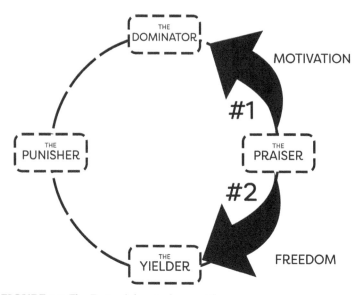

**FIGURE 2.9** The Praiser's hemisphere outflows

*I'm taking care of you, motivating and hand holding. (#1)* They did a great job but need continued motivating structure; I don't anticipate my student/s slipping, but I know I will be spending a lot of time ensuring they don't. Typical signals include appreciation, a sense of insecurity, a need for more time and care, openness to receive motivation, a desire for mentorship and supervised challenges.

*Go! Be free! And assume more responsibility for your outcomes! (#2)* Wow, I couldn't be any prouder of them. They totally "get it." I'm so happy about their achievements that I am willing to send them to create, expand, and explore! Usual signals include a desire for adventure, welcoming risks, confidence, need for creativity, optimism, and responsibility.

## Teaching The Geometry Class

Mya's killing it with her proofs, but she needs a high level of motivation. I'm working with her a lot, enjoying mentoring and guiding her, and watching her continuously grow. In the back of my mind, I sense she's telling me to break this loop and send her from motivation to freedom.

Bix just can't understand the concept of geometry proofing, and no matter how I explain it, he can't get it. I've sent him videos, tutored him, and used more metaphors for theorems than I can count. He's pretty upset. He keeps saying, "My mind just doesn't work that way!" We're in a needy loop, but I am confident an "aha" signal will show up soon.

(The star shows how I framed for both students and the gray arrows show my intentions.)

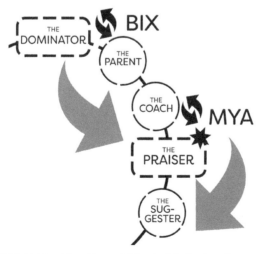

**FIGURE 2.10** Teaching Bix and Mya in Motivation flows as I play The Praiser

## Visualize

1.  Think about times when you found yourself in a flows loop you knew you needed to break.
2.  Identify ramifications for breaking flows loops too soon or too late.
3.  Explain how an awareness of flows loops can benefit students and improve your teaching.

---

### Teaching The Shop Class

Bix found himself in a world of bliss as he hand-planes his emerging lamp base. Until recently, Bix perpetuated as one the most challenging students to teach until he found his calling with woodwork, presenting me with surprising and welcome responsibility and freedom signals. Bix approaches, "Hey, what do you think of my lamp so far?" I respond, "I think it looks amazing. This one area here looks like you're going a bit too much against the grain." I loved Bix's response that confirmed my signal interpretations: "Yeah, I meant it to be like that in that spot." With Bix, I'll look for the "more challenge, please" signal.

Mya, the creative, carved three wooden spoons, preparing the wood burner to add some decoration. She asks, "Teacher, can you demonstrate how to use this burner thing one more time?" As I turn on the tool, I respond, "Sure, Mya, what will you do with these neato spoons?" Mya: My boyfriend's mom's birthday is next week, and I'm going to give these to her for my present,"—I decide to briefly play The

Friend when I finish the demonstration, ending with, "Fantastic! Well, Tell Harry, 'Hi,' and send happy birthday wishes from me to his mom," From experience with natural creatives like Mya, I'll watch usual signals such as sudden boredom, need for new challenges, and a wish to change spaces.

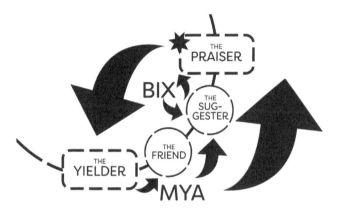

**FIGURE 2.11** Teaching Bix and Mya in Freedom flows as I frame with The Praiser

### *Visualize*

How would (or do) you interact with enthused students who love what they're doing and need the freedom to create and grow? Explain specific ways you take action to bolster their success.

## Hope and Freedom from The Yielder's Perspective

I'm testing my student's/s' skills and readiness, preparing them for independent thinking and creativity. This flow's hemisphere may appear easy to teach in since I will not be around very much or even at all; I occasionally get accused by some students who expect to be closely managed of "not doing my job." However, effectively flowing in and out of parts in this hemisphere requires the highest teaching skill level. Most difficulty involves providing the illusion of "monitoring without monitoring." I always know what's happening and perform quality control, even when I'm entirely away. This hemisphere is where magical flows often happen, and, in a perfect world where all students produce great work and remain perpetually motivated, I could stay down here forever.

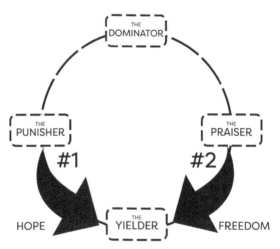

**FIGURE 2.12** The Yielder's hemisphere inflows

*I'm creating an atmosphere of exhilaration or stunned hope. (#1)* I'm generally leaving the students alone to work, optimistic they'll achieve big success! I will be sure to keep out of their way and not spoil a good thing. I'm primarily bouncing between the Drilling Parts; however, sometimes The Punisher will send student/s to me who didn't meet behavior or learning outcomes. (I'm testing them, and they are shocked by the sudden freedom and generally hands-off atmosphere they've suddenly been thrust into.) Expected signals I sense and see: hope, risk, responsibility, a "try me/test me" attitude, confidence, excitement, creativity, a desire to explore, and variable levels of optimism, shock, and disorientation. Some students may express anxiety over being let go so completely.

*Welcome to independence! (#2)* Here comes a bunch of competent, excited, creative, and ready students whose minds have been lit on fire, preparing to be independently productive, and I'm getting out of their way to rev up the electric learning atmosphere even more. Common signals I sense and see include justified high confidence, respect, joy, embrace of risk, highest responsibility, an "I'll show you how I can do amazing things" attitude, massive excitement, creativity, a desire to explore, willingness to receive feedback to improve, highest possible student optimism, and minds ablaze.

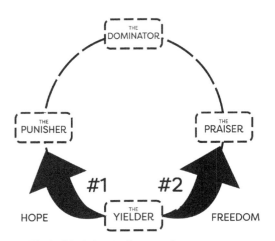

**FIGURE 2.13** The Yielder's hemisphere outflows

*I'm challenging them to find out and explore on their own. (#1)* I'm setting them up, and now I'm letting them go—with a lot of hope. I hope they will do great work and be ready to steer their learning process from a distance, but I'll still be nearby when they need me. Although this hemisphere flow's relationship with The Punisher, who shares this Hope Quad with me, is aloof at best, I only expect to play Hope Quad parts; I know some students may continue up to the tough love part of the wheel. I always need to keep a distant eye out for any abuse of freedom and watch for potential irresponsibility. Standard signals include a "test me out" attitude, a desire for adventure, challenge, deserved confidence, over-confidence, craving creativity, discovery, optimism, responsibility, and, as mentioned, irresponsibility.

*I'm celebrating their massive self-directed productivity. (#2)* I'm letting them fly. Most will show me the amazing things they created and tell me how much they learned and grew. Common signals include thankfulness, achievement, excitement, accomplishment, happiness, responsibility, pride, and "let's do-more-to-make-it-better creativity."

---

### The Architectural Rendering Software Lab

Far ahead of everyone else still learning the basics of the rendering software, I've informally reviewed Bix's spectacular building elevations he created on app functions I'm teaching today. I'm sensing Bix doesn't need me anymore; he needs me to meet him at his skill level. I must get him out of here immediately—he shouldn't listen to more directions on this. I called him up. *Me:* "Bix, get out of here. Go wherever you want – home even. Instead of wasting time waiting for others to catch up with you, make a few more snazzy renderings and send the files to me to look at tonight." Bix just smiled, grabbed his stuff, and left.

I'm not sure what's going on with Mya, and I'm watching her from across the lab space. I can see by the look on her face she's stuck. I wait a few more minutes before I decide to rescue her.

*Me:* "How's it going, Mya?" Mya looks at me with telltale "Thanks for your help!" relieved eyes. *Mya:* "Hi. As you can see, I'm a bit hung up. I can't find the shortcut keys for the render function." (I know Mya's generally a conscientious student, and I am shocked.) *Me:* "Mya, I explained this over and over in the instructions to the class before the lab period began." I sit down next to her. *Me:* "You'd think the most important function would be front and center, easy to see. Here it is."

As I returned to my previous spot, I noticed Mya opening a window on her computer screen and began browsing (well, probably returning to browse) a shopping website.

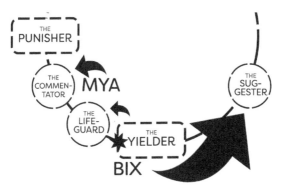

**FIGURE 2.14** Teaching Bix and Mya in very different ways

*Visualize*

Think about Bix's exceptional knowledge and skills. How do you take action when a student knows much more than the rest of the class? Do you make them wait on the others to catch up, or do you find ways to keep them going? Would you choose to differentiate students who love what they're doing and need the freedom to create and grow? What would the next scene be in your visualization with obviously slacking Mya?

## Motivation and Tough Love from The Dominator's Perspective

These flows are serious business because framing with The Dominator makes me feel the weight of my decisions and responsibility to my students. I'm perpetually hard-leaning toward being able to send and receive flows to and from The Praiser. All of these parts require me to be most physically active and mentally aware as I establish and maintain control of my student/s, constantly pushing and pulling them toward the right or bottom hemispheres.

*I must control, and I am controlling! (#1)* I hope to see good progress, but even if I do, I dare not lose a scintilla of control since I'm losing confidence in their will to do the work. Common signals I'm sensing and seeing include the need for structure, low respect, anger, overt and covert anxiousness, irresponsibility, and optimism for redemption.

*I'm prepared to begin requiring strict oversight. (#2)* I feel alert and ready because the student/s need me to

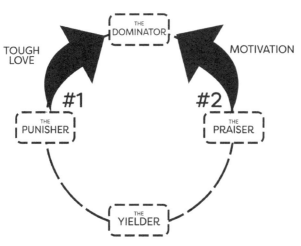

**FIGURE 2.15** The Dominator's hemisphere inflows

take command, so I prepare new strategies for establishing power and control. I sense and see usual signals including thankfulness for needed structure, low tolerance for risk, and irresponsibility.

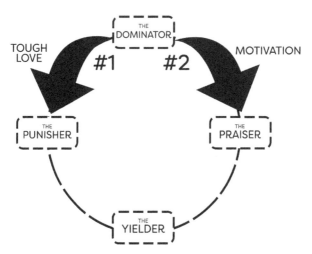

**FIGURE 2.16** The Dominator's hemisphere outflows

*I'm in emergency control mode! (#1)* I hope this flow is more like a short course correction instead of a cliff, depending on the student's/s' attitude and willingness to meet my clear standards. Signals I'm sensing and seeing include lack of understanding of the subject, thankfulness for my watchful eye, low expectations for accomplishment, irresponsibility, and lack of pride. This flow may not be enjoyable to me, but it is vital for keeping learning integrity, my professionalism, and honoring the students who work hard and do their best.

*I'm providing personalized care. (#2)* This could be great for their progress! I'm doing a lot of heavy lifting, but I can sense new potential in the student's/s' attitude and motivation going in the right direction. Typical signals I'm sensing and seeing include sudden buoyancy, industrial and intellectual poise, and an expectation for incremental achievement. I hope all this time and effort I'm spending pays off.

---

### Visualize

Craft a teaching story in your mind about two students flowing in different directions. One student slips fast toward potential failure; the other sees promise and possibility. Watch yourself interact with them and notice the choices you make.

---

## Hope and Tough Love from the Punisher's Perspective

Left hemisphere flows represent multifaceted, seemingly disparate parts whose connections might not make sense to people unfamiliar with what students often require educators to do: combine tough love with hope. When I frame with The Punisher, I'm likely flowing toward The Dominator since administering punishment does not usually raise my trust levels. However, Hope (Quad) flows become useful when circumstances call for offering student/s space to cool off or provide reflective challenges.

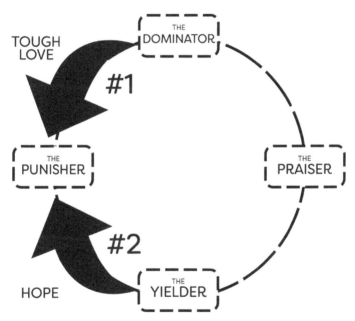

**FIGURE 2.17** The Punisher's hemisphere inflows

*I'm watching a potential disaster happen. (#1)* I'm on guard for holding students accountable for negative consequences for unmet outcomes. (I'm trying hard not to let this happen, of course.) Usual signals include dread, lethargy, apathy, sustained cynicism, confusion, and exhaustion.

*Really? (#2)* This is an unusual flow because I rarely need to punish people basking in hope, but those I do deserve consequences for their malfeasance. Usual signals I sense and see in both flows include irresponsibility, sudden apathy, unexpected and surprising cynicism, lack of respect, a chance given and lost, and panic.

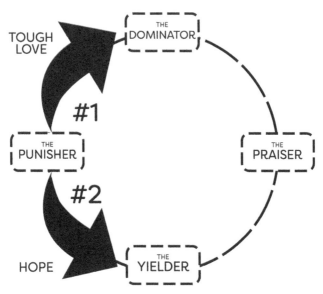

**FIGURE 2.18** The Punisher's hemisphere outflows

*I'm tending to them after their fall. (#1)* I'm sending the students/s back to structure and praying for the best! Common signals I sense and see include anger, disappointment, sarcasm, irresponsibility, thankfulness, alertness, apathy, and (potentially) exhaustion.

*I'm offering a chance for redemption. (#2)* My students need flexibility and to reflect after being penalized, and I'm offering them grace and mercy. Typical signals I sense and see include a desire for redemption, respect, thankfulness, restlessness, newfound confidence, optimism, and challenge.

## Bix's Glitter and Glue Art Exhibition

Bix! In the time it took for me to conclude my short conversation with the principal (only one step out in the hall and barely out of sight of my students), Bix took his opportunity. Every bottle of school glue I set out only minutes ago was now empty with their contents embedded deep in carpet fibers. He dumped all the glitter on the glue, rolled around in it, and by the time I turned around, Bix, shimmering with glitter, glistening under the glow of my room's bright fluorescent lights, presented himself as a human glitter and glue art installation.

ME: "Bix! What in the world!"
BIX: "Look! I'm a shiny statue!"

After I washed and dried him off, I didn't punish him even though I was in a punishing mindset. It occurred to me Bix's misbehavior could be considered a burst of creative ingenuity and spontaneous expression; he just couldn't resist.

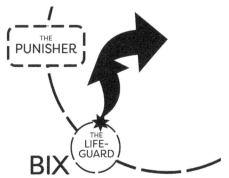

FIGURE 2.19 An illogical flow for Bix

> ### Visualize Illogical Flow Diversions
>
> Interacting with human beings requires breaking logic. Sometimes your educational intuition prohibits punishment, as happened in an unsteady flow caused by Bix. Think about situations when you will need to make instant diversions. Praise often takes the place of punishment in my teaching, and I expect it does for yours, too. Why is this important? What happens when you decide not to divert, sticking to logic?

# Smooth Flows

Finding myself in a smooth teaching flow feels like jazz; I'm free to improvise and explore, kind of like free-form scatting, though I realize the massive structure and skill it takes. Smooth teaching flows resemble an airplane ride in clear skies and no turbulence and riding on ocean waves that gently roll under my raft. I rarely experienced this smooth flow rhythm until I first became aware of my parts so I could recognize and understand their connections.

The best example of my smooth flows happens when I teach in and near my Freedom Quad, especially in a Yielder-Lifeguard-Yielder-Suggester-Praiser-Friend-Yielder flow. By the way: when I wrote this long flow name, I laughed out loud! It was the first time I ever wrote out any of my flows in words, and I would never use this compound-parts term in practice. (Neither should you!) The diagrams say it all, and writing this flow out reminded me again of the complexities of teaching and the value of drawing to understand what we do as teachers.

# Jarring Flows

An abrupt shift in the tone of a classroom or one-on-one interaction, "Jarring Flows," can be beneficial when a signal demands instant, substantial changes. I expect big eyes, blank or surprised faces (depending on the situation), stunned silence or gasps, clapping, shrieking, catching a deep breath, alertness, playfulness, or seriousness (among other strong reactions), with suddenly different air filling the classroom. Jarring Flows connect one Framing Part to another directly across the wheel, moving my teaching tone into a completely opposite feel, changing the student's/s' experiences.

My most common jarring flow includes *The Dominator to The Yielder*. In this case, I either know to shift when I detect a sudden rise in my student's/s' readiness or if I need to test whether I should have confidence in their knowledge or gauge if they can or will take responsibility for their learning.

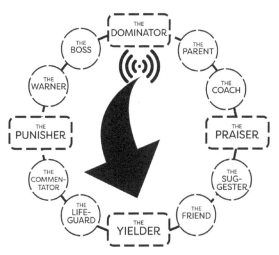

**FIGURE 2.20** The jolting Dominator-to-Yielder flow

The Yielder-to-The Dominator's jarring flow occurs when I spot a signal letting me know that my students suddenly need a controlled redirect. Though essential to maintaining integrity in my teaching and a significant, indispensable flow that I must play, I don't enjoy it: I like when I can set student/s free to create and invent, but when I do, sometimes they renege, miss a critical deadline, don't know the material as much as I thought they did, or they didn't bother to show up—I discovered new information or misinterpreted their capabilities, desire to learn, or skill level.

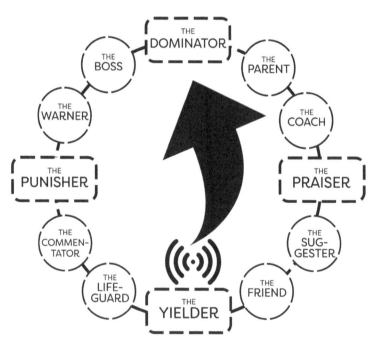

**FIGURE 2.21** The breathtaking Yielder-to-Dominator redirect

Another reasonably common Jarring Flow, The Punisher-Praiser, happens when a signal jolts with the brilliance of achievement suddenly met. This shift also happens in spontaneous surprises, a good news break in a time of trial.

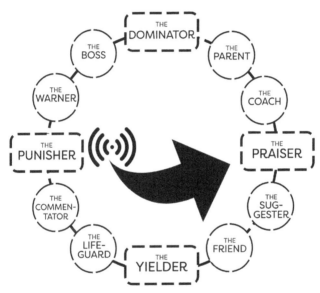

**FIGURE 2.22** The surprised, ecstatic experience of the Punisher-to-Praiser flow

The Praiser to The Penalizer represents an unfamiliar jarring flow and terrible teaching. I cannot think of a scenario where I would frame with joy and celebration followed immediately by a corrective tone. Although I can't understand how this flow could be considered acceptable teaching practice, I include it here if you can.

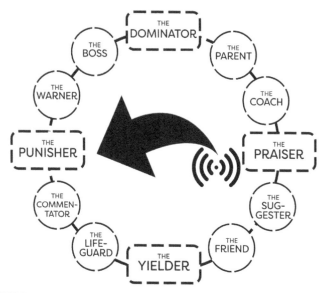

**FIGURE 2.23** The generally nonexistent (and horrible teaching!) Praiser-to-Penalizer flow

Cross-hemisphere flows help my teaching, but it took a while for me to use them effectively. I believe knowing how to make these connections seamlessly powers my classroom and implementing them could be the biggest reason for my teaching career's success.

### You, a Student Experiencing a Flow Jolt

Visualize yourself back when you were a student. Did you ever experience a jolt when you were taking a class that seemed to flow very smoothly? What happened? How did it feel? What was the impact? Why do you think the flow needed to shift?

# No Flows and Many Signals

Most educators understand teaching flows whether or not they know the terminology in this book. Since flows connect the parts you play, you can map those connections and evaluate your flow strings. When teachers don't know about or ignore their flows, they leave their teaching effectiveness up to chance, sometimes with dreadful outcomes.

A timeless example of understanding the impacts of "flows and signals ignorance" occurs in the 1986 movie *Ferris Bueller's Day Off*. In the enduring classroom scene, Mr. Lorensax, Ferris' teacher, calls the attendance roll in a robotic voice (and with his hilarious lifeless facial expression), "Bueller? Bueller? … Bueller?" before lecturing a class of high school students. Mr. Lorensax only played one part with no flows (flows can't connect parts when a teacher only plays one). He ignored many otherwise easy-to-spot signals (overt student boredom, pointed hostility, checking out, drooling, heads on desks, eyes rolled

---

### Visualize

Many more famous examples of educators not paying attention to flows exist. I think of Peanuts' Charlie Brown's "wah-wah" teacher and Mr. Hand from the movie Fast Times at Ridgemont High. I can easily recall several one-part, no-flow teachers over my student years, and I'll bet you can, too. What was the one part they played? Describe the signals they missed. Have you ever caught yourself teaching this way? (I have!)

back or crossed, and carefree sleeping). By choosing not to respond to the many obvious signals and not connecting to new parts, it is reasonable to conclude Mr. Lorensax's students likely failed to achieve expected learning outcomes, one of the best movie scenes illustrating how not to teach!

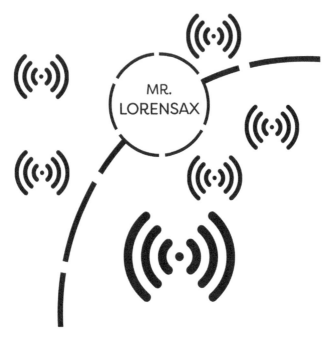

**FIGURE 2.24** Mr. Lorensax's one part. No flows. Lots of signals!

## Before You Leave Chapter 2

You've covered parts in Chapter 1, and flows and signals in Chapter 2. Now take some time to reflect on *your* parts, flows, and signals to prepare you for the next chapter, where you'll begin drawing them!

## Parts, Flows, and Signals Reflection

Ask yourself, "What is my...

- ◆ most effective part and why it works so well for my students?"
- ◆ least effective part and why it doesn't work well?"
- ◆ most enjoyable part to play and why it's so much fun?
- ◆ least enjoyable part to play and why it's painful for me?
- ◆ part or parts from the book I don't play or agree with?
- ◆ part or parts not included in the book I added based on my self-observation?
- ◆ funniest or most unusual part I play?
- ◆ smoothest flow: why it feels so smooth when I play it?
- ◆ most effective flow and why it works so well for my students?
- ◆ clunkiest or most jarring flow and its (positive or negative) effect?
- ◆ least effective flow?
- ◆ most sensed and seen signal?
- ◆ least sensed and seen signal?
- ◆ most positively impactful signal?
- ◆ least positively impactful signal?
- ◆ most surprising or startling signal?
- ◆ unique style of teaching described in a term or a sentence?
- ◆ unique style of teaching, and how does it impact my students?

Reflect on …

◆ a scenario where you experience your best teaching flows (connections). Explain if these connections put you "in flow" or "in your teaching zone." How do you feel when you teach in this flow? What signals do you associate with it? How do your students feel? What benefits do students receive when you teach this way?

◆ your idea of flows representing "bad teaching." What does "bad teaching" mean to you, and what contributions do flows make?

◆ parts and flows that might not be enjoyable for you in your practice but are necessary for impactful teaching. What drove your decisions in choosing these?

# Final Thoughts on Flows and Signals

*Nice work!*

You have a solid handle on the concept of flows and signals. In this chapter, you learned what a flow is and how teaching flows are directly related to being "in flow" or "in the zone" as a teacher. You completed a flows boot camp where you learned how Quad Flows work and how they combine adjacent Quad Flows to make Hemisphere Flows. In that lesson, I showed you how the nuances of your teaching can be understood by knowing your inflows and outflows and how they relate to your Framing Parts.

You learned about smooth, jarring, and "no flows" and why understanding these are so important.

Now, go on to Chapter 3 to visualize your teaching through self-observation and diagramming your parts, flows, and signals.

# Reference

Csikszentmihalyi, M. (1997). *Finding flow: the psychology of engagement with everyday life* (Vol. 37). New York, NY: Basic Books.

# 3

# "See," Then Draw (or Doodle) Your Teaching (with 10 Teaching Stories)

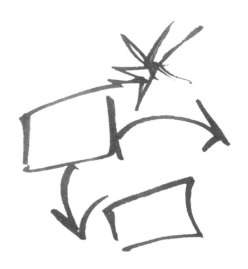

DOI: 10.4324/9781003360230-4

> Drawing your teaching creates powerful revelations, and if you keep an open mind, it can positively change your craft forever. *And fast!* Just as it did for me.

*Great work so far!*

Now it's time to draw! (Or doodle!) Put your learning into practice by visualizing and diagramming. Ten scenarios feature diagrams I created to launch your imagination, including previous and future teaching stories with instructions to help you build fruitful self-observations.

Please follow these instructions:

- ◆ "See" yourself teaching as *you*. Do not act differently or behave uncharacteristically. Remember, you are self-observing the existing conditions of your teaching!
- ◆ You'll need something to draw on.
- ◆ Decide what drawing utensils you will use.
- ◆ Prepare to take notes of what you're seeing.
- ◆ Don't worry about how your drawings look.
- ◆ Start your diagrams with my wheel shape, followed by the rectangles for the Framing Parts and circles for the Drilling Parts on the wheel. Then add the flows, connect the parts, and sprinkle in the signals where they show up. Or choose another way to draw if something works better for you than my wheel, arrows, and shapes. My method doesn't have to be yours; the thinking is the point, the drawing, the means.
- ◆ Make sure that if you see your drawings years from now, you will always be able to know what each

represents; consider including notes and descriptive labels.

♦ Written minimally by design, scenario descriptions require you to add the specifics.

♦ Notice detailed instructions in the first two scenarios aren't offered in the rest to encourage you to set up teaching stories independently as you become more confident in your visualization skills.

♦ Though I see the parts I feature as universal to the teaching profession; I encourage you to push back! This chapter offers an opportunity to consider how you might modify them, change their names to match your teaching circumstances and style, and create new ones as you see fit based on those you identify in your teaching.

♦ *Have fun with this!* Visualizing and drawing should be a joyous experience that shouldn't feel bogged down. Let the energy flow as you learn more about yourself as a teacher.

*Let's get started!*

# #1: Teach Susan with Her Mind Suddenly on Fire

BING-BING-BING! Susan suddenly "gets it"—*big time!*
   Instructions:

*Visualize <u>yesterday's class</u> when you taught Susan.*

1. *Make up a teaching story about teaching Susan yesterday.* What was her assignment or project? Why

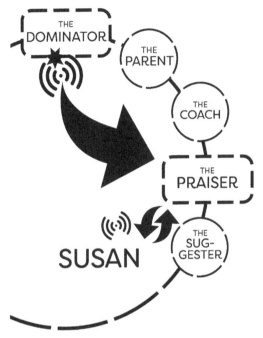

**FIGURE 3.1** Yesterday's class with Susan

was it so hard for her? How long was she confused? Create the context for what Susan "gets" and develop a compelling background story of how she struggled to understand something.

2. *Now "See" Susan.* What subjects does she love? Hate? Think about her skills and her limitations. How would you describe your relationship with her? What does she think about this class? How does she see you? Describe her attitude. Do you know if she has any dreams or ambitions? Now think more meta: of all people in the universe, why did she appear in your life, and, since she is, identify your specific purpose meant to help her learn and grow.

3. *Next, create the educational setting with Susan. Notice the space where you taught Susan yesterday.* Think back to when you sat in the empty classroom waiting for her. Look around. What did you see? What did you hear? Did the space have detailed textures? How did the classroom smell? Describe how the room generally felt. How did *you* feel?

4. *Now create the full, rich scene describing how you taught Susan yesterday.* Notice how you began framing as The Dominator (see page 36) and watched yourself interact with Susan through the class period's flows. Recall the instant the strong signal popped up at the beginning of your engagement [her moment of clarity]. Then, recall the experience when you lurched to play The Praiser (see page 31) and describe the impacts of your response decisions. Think about how happy you both felt when you threw her into a flows loop with The Suggester (see page 61) and The Praiser. Explain how your decisions advanced her ideas, improving her work on this assignment.

5. *Think about the ending of your engagement with Susan yesterday.* Describe the feelings you and Susan experienced as you ended your interaction when you framed as The Praiser. What circumstances created those feelings? Explain Susan's attitude and posture as she exited. Think about why your decision to end this way was important. Finally, see the empty learning space again, without Susan.

6. *"Summarize and say" to build your teaching muscle memory.* Describe the general tempo of your exchange with her over the engagement. What was the volume of your interaction? Did you move?

How? To and from where? And for what purpose? Describe your posture and mannerisms during your time with Susan yesterday. Then, select a word, a term, or write a sentence summarizing "the feeling" of yesterday's overall experience. Say it out loud to etch this engagement with Susan into your concentrated experience so you can draw on it when you teach in real life!

*Diagram today's class teaching Susan.*

1. *Notice your space today.* Skip this if you decide to stay in the same area as you did yesterday, but if somewhere else, situate yourself in the new space. It's empty right now. Look around. What do you see? What do you hear? Does the area have detailed textures? How does it smell? How does it feel? How do *you* feel?

2. *"See" Susan's change in today's class.* Does she have a different demeanor than yesterday? What actions tell you she's different today? How are *you* different today?

3. *Establish an overall feeling you will create with Susan in class today.* What tempo will you maintain? Will your voice need to change in any way? How loud or soft will you be when working face-to-face with her? Will you move? How? To and from where? And why? What will your mannerisms suggest to Susan? How will implementing these presets establish the overall feeling of your interaction? Describe that feeling.

4. *Now develop a full, rich scene teaching Susan today—and draw it!* There is no diagram to study

to guide how you create your teaching experience today—it's your turn to take the knowledge and skills you learned in this book to this point and create your own drawing. How will you frame your time with Susan today? How did you make progress? Does Susan continue improving or experience a snag? Carefully tell the story with which parts you will play and the context associated with these decisions and draw their connections. What signals will pop up? [Maybe the signals are fainter and more nuanced than yesterday's sudden epiphany.] Where will you take Susan today? How will you end the scene?

5. *"Summarize and say" to build your teaching muscle memory.* Now, select a word, a term, or write a sentence summarizing "the feeling" of your experience teaching Susan today. Say it out loud to etch it in your mind.

# #2: Flailing Team B

Team B's work fell apart! They appeared to be on track at first (Notice the gray-shaded flows from yesterday's class), but their substandard work required a new direction. Today (see the black-shaded flows), unfortunately, they continued to veer off track.

*Visualize when you taught Team B <u>yesterday</u>.*

1. *Make up a teaching story about teaching Team B yesterday.* Decide on their assignment or project. Notice how you framed the interaction first as The

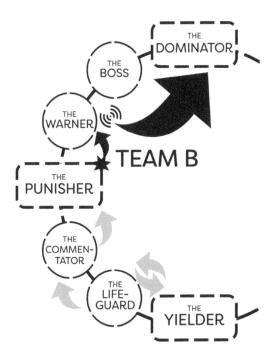

**FIGURE 3.2** Team B's freefall yesterday (flows in gray) and today's interesting class period

Yielder (page 34) to establish an atmosphere of creativity and exploration. What background story explains why you decided to frame this way at the beginning?

2. *Now "See" each member of Team B.* How many students comprise this team? Who are they? How old are they? What do they look like? Give them names. What do they love? Hate? Think about their skills and limitations. How would you describe your relationship with them? What do they think about this class? How do they see you? Describe their attitudes. Describe their general attitude as a team. Do you

know if any of them have particular dreams or ambitions? Now think more meta: of all people in the universe, why did these people appear in your life, and, since they did, identify your specific purpose meant to help them learn and grow.

3. *Notice the space.* You taught Team B in a different setting than where you interacted with Susan in the previous scenario, so describe this space before they arrived yesterday. Look around. What did you see? What did you hear? Did the area have particular textures? How did the space smell? How did it feel? How did *you* feel?

4. *Start framing as The Yielder.* Team B arrived, and you started teaching. Did everyone show up? How did you begin your interaction with them? Please explain how you set up a hopeful and free learning atmosphere. What did you mean by "hopeful" in Team B's assignment context? How did you provide instructions to them? How did you make them appreciate and be excited about the trust you bestowed?

5. *Tell the full, rich story of you teaching Team B yesterday*. Move through the flows as you stop playing The Yielder and watch yourself guide Team B through the other parts. At first, you placed them in a high hope loop—The Yielder to The Lifeguard (page 51)—but they somehow lost their way. What happened? Imagine the elements guiding your decision to flow from The Commentator (see page 45) to The Punisher (page 39). Watch members of Team B's interactions over the flows. How would you explain their weaknesses and strengths? Do you detect any attitudes? How would you describe the tempo of your interactions? What was the volume of

your exchange? Did it vary over the period? Did you move? How? To and from where? And why? Describe your posture and mannerisms during your time with Team B yesterday.

6. *Think about the unfortunate ending in yesterday's class with Team B.* Ending with The Punisher must have been an unpleasant (but necessary) scene. Why couldn't you find a way to hard shift to The Praiser, framing the ending more positively, especially after finishing as The Punisher yesterday? Tell the story and describe the scene as Team B exits the class.

7. *Summarize yesterday's experience with Team B to contribute to your teaching "muscle memory."* Now, select a word, a term, or write a sentence describing "the feeling" of your teaching experience yesterday. Say it out loud.

*Visualize yourself teaching Team B <u>today</u>.*

1. *Notice your space.* Get acquainted if it's a new room or area than where you taught yesterday. Empty now, see what's there, hear any sounds, feel textures, and notice smells. How does it feel? How do *you* feel?

2. *Make up a teaching story about teaching Team B today. Initially frame as The Punisher, a rare, unfortunate situation.* (They gave you no choice.) Team B arrives. How will you start your interaction with them? See yourself on the approach. Did everyone show up? Are they still working on the same assignment or project? Describe the atmosphere in detail.

3. *Tell the full, rich story of you teaching Team B today.* Black arrows describe the flows of today's class. Start them working. Watch members of Team B interact. What are they working on? How are they working

together? Notice ways the team seems different today. Do you detect any team members or members who have changed since yesterday? If you did, describe how. You continue as The Warner (see page 59), indicating continued loss of trust and requiring more hands-on teaching, where you received a signal. What signal caused you to end today's class framing as The Dominator? Review why and how you played each part and examine your decisions for choosing to connect them. How would you describe the tempo of your interactions? What was the volume? Did you move? How? To and from where? And why? Describe your posture and mannerisms during your time with them yesterday.

4. *Think about how Team B left today.* Ending the class framing with The Dominator established a much different feeling than yesterday's finish playing The Punisher. Explain these differences.

5. *Summarize your experience with Team B to contribute to your teaching "muscle memory."* Write it. Say it out loud.

*Visualize and draw <u>tomorrow's</u> class teaching Team B.*

1. *Notice your space.*
2. *Decide which Framing Part you'll play at the beginning of the class.* Why did you choose this frame? How does it correspond to the frame from today's lesson?
3. *Tell a story of Team B's progress <u>tomorrow</u>.* What happens to them? Do they reach milestones? Can you single out any individual on the team who became leaders? Did any members of the team hold back progress? Did you steer them toward the Motivation

Quad, or are they stuck in Tough Love (page 66)? Did you implement any Jarring Flows (page 117), or did you stick with flowing logically? How does tomorrow's teaching story end? How do you frame the ending?

4. *Diagram!*

---

**Letting You Fly!**

The remaining eight scenarios include only short descriptions and no instructions. Use what you learned to design your own rich teaching stories for deep self-reflection to enhance your collective experience. Remember, make this fun and effortless!

---

# #3: Connie. Friend or Educator? Teach Her Next Class

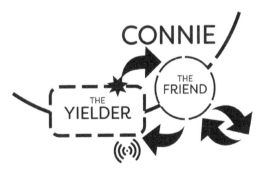

**FIGURE 3.3** Casual for a long time today with Connie

In today's class, Connie couldn't get serious, and you stayed informal with her for a very long time. What tack will you take with her next? In detail, diagram and reflect on teaching Connie's next class.

## #4 Samir's Epiphany Today Set Me in Motion

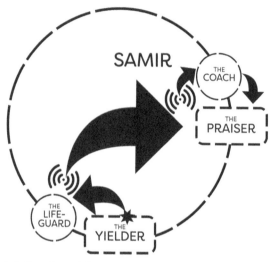

**FIGURE 3.4** Signals proliferated when teaching Samir <u>yesterday</u>

Observe yourself teaching Samir yesterday when he revealed a positive attitude and willingness to risk. He created a masterpiece deliverable that caused you to jump in with force to improve his work. Continue the story by drawing what happened <u>today</u>, and then make another diagram of his <u>journey tomorrow</u>. Reflect as you go.

## #5: Teaching Ambitious Amber and Joyous Jonie

Two-member team Amber and Jonie couldn't contain their excitement when they hit a breakthrough on their project <u>this week</u>, and you sent them away to explore and improve

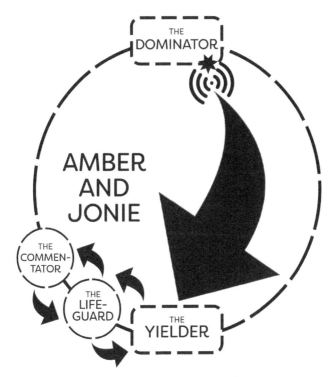

**FIGURE 3.5** This was quite a <u>week</u> for Amber and Jonie

on their own. Tell the background story by drawing what happened with them <u>last week</u>. After you complete last week's illustration, forecast their progress over the <u>next week</u> with another general drawing.

## #6: Send a Positive Jolt into the Classroom

You sensed and responded to a signal and "hard flowed" your class out of a quickly negative downward spiral, hoping the shift in tone will inspire your students to become

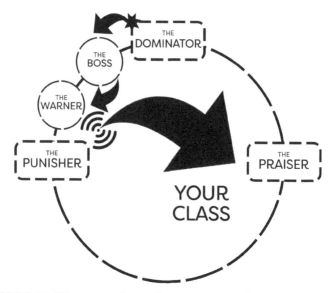

**FIGURE 3.6** What a complete and utter disaster <u>today</u>. Something HAD to change

more responsible and decide to do the work. Create a story describing what happened in today's class, then describe the strong signal that made you decide on such a jarring flow change. <u>Diagram tomorrow's class</u>.

## #7: All They Needed Was a Little TLC

It only took five minutes after the start of today's class discussion to realize your students did not do their reading homework, unable to contribute effectively. Tell today's story of your teaching and create a drawing that shows how class discussions play out <u>tomorrow</u>.

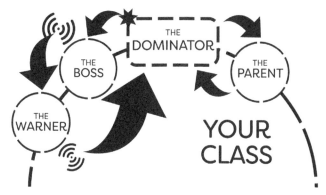

FIGURE 3.7 Just a little love at the end of class did the trick today

## #8: Amna-in-the Zone

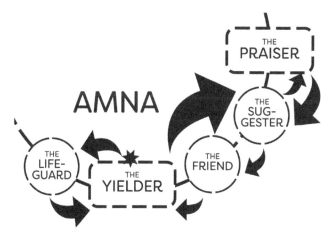

FIGURE 3.8 Today's class shows Amna's incredible journey

Notice Amna's productive flows, illustrating her substantial progress today. Tell the story of Amna's inspired experience, and watch yourself guide her as you diagram what happened yesterday.

## #9: Try to Encourage Jittery Jim

After framing with The Praiser, assess how Jim responds to your careful mentoring directives today and how he's losing confidence and needs more attention. Tell the more detailed story of your interaction with Jim <u>tomorrow and the following day's exchanges</u>.

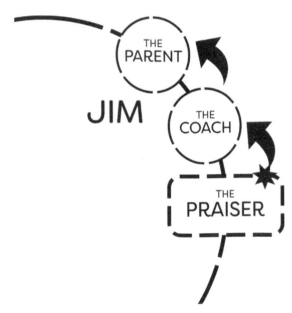

**FIGURE 3.9** <u>Today</u> with Jittery Jim

## #10: I Tried Hard Directing Team D!

Use your growing teaching visualization skills to study Team D's overall experience for <u>this month</u> and create a story and a diagram about Team D's progress <u>last month</u>.

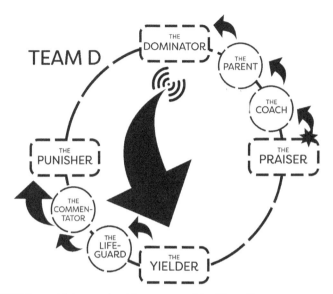

**FIGURE 3.10** <u>This month</u> with ever-morphing Team D

## Bonus Diagram

Your first week as a teacher didn't go very well, but you rocked it the following week! Study and tell the story of your unfortunate teaching <u>last week,</u> and then diagram your comparably fabulous <u>second week</u> after discovering parts, flows, and signals!

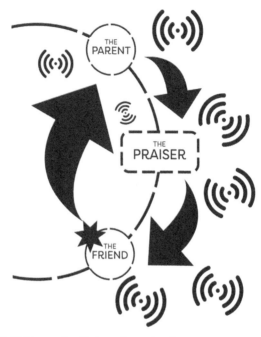

**FIGURE 3.11** Your naive first week as a teacher

*Congratulations!*

Now you have a better awareness of your teaching style—your unique brand as an educator. Your heightened educational intuition has already strengthened your practice and transformed your teaching. Keep going! Keep visualizing and diagramming until you know you don't need to anymore. *You'll be shocked how soon that moment will come!*

# Afterword
## Go Forth and Prosper!

I realized from the beginning how weird this book is. Most teaching books offer step-by-step lesson-plan-based templates, but this book's impractical—(impossible!) "template" of teaching parts, flows, and signals cannot (and should not) be taken into a classroom and expected to be systematically implemented in real time, such as in "Okay, now I'm playing The Yielder," and in ten minutes, I know I'll flow to The Praiser, then watch for a signal ..."

*See?*

The point I hope you take away: *Know your teaching like the back of your hand.* Build an awareness trove of possibilities and probabilities to activate automatic decision-making and how the decisions impact your students.

Remember the metaphor I used about this book being your "batting cage?" Softball players standing at the plate ready to swing do not bring a list directing how they plan to hit the ball because they don't know—*until they know*—what kind of pitch will be coming!

I never consciously think about parts, flows, and signals anymore and haven't for a very long time. I don't need to! Teaching intuition will soon be a part of your practice, too. Prepare to become equipped for immediately flexing in any situation with ready-to-go experience waiting to deploy.

Thank you for taking this peculiar journey with me. I am confident that if you stepped through this book, your chances are excellent for becoming the best teacher in your building or campus. Your students will appreciate it.

For Product Safety Concerns and Information please contact our
EU representative GPSR@taylorandfrancis.com Taylor & Francis
Verlag GmbH, Kaufingerstraße 24, 80331 München, Germany